Romance without kisses.

By Terry Basson

Cepia Books

PUBLISHED BY CEPIA BOOKS

Copyright © Terry Basson, 2011.

The moral right of Terry Basson to be identified as the author of this work has been asserted by him in accordance with the Copyright, Designs and Patents Act of 1988.

All rights reserved. No part of this publication may be reproduced, stored in a retrieval system or transmitted in any form or by any means, electronic, mechanical, photocopying, recording or otherwise, without the prior permission of the copyright owner.

ISBN 978 1 908016 07 2

(Cover photograph copyright © Terry Basson.)

Typeset by Redegg Solutions, Bath.
www.redeggsolutions.co.uk

Printed and bound in the UK by Imprint digital, Exeter.

Cepia Books
19 Garstons, Bathford, Bath BA1 7TE

www.cepiabooks.co.uk

Foreword

I wanted to write about my wartime childhood (1939 –1945) and tell my Basson family and friends all about it. In the end, I have included pieces about my life, National Service and my life at work.

This story is also a tribute to Mum and Dad and their lives during difficult times. Sadly all my siblings have passed this life now, so I felt it vital to leave my record of how things were long ago.

To my son David, I must say a big thank you for giving me my first computer which has, since my retirement, encouraged me to write. David's skills as a Graphic Designer have produced this book for me. During this time I have sat beside him in his studio realising what a clever and talented man he is. Splendid Dave!

I also acknowledge the many dedicated hours Di has spent, nudging and encouraging me throughout months of preparation.

I do so hope you enjoy these shared memories.

Terry Basson

Contents

1	Me and how it was	1
2	The skies over London in 1939	9
3	We moved and Dad joined up	13
4	Pop's café	19
5	A child in Woodbridge	29
6	VE Day (Victory in Europe)	37
7	Return to London	41
8	A Yank returns much later on	51
9	Saxmundham	63
10	First steps into the world of work	73
11	National Service	79
12	Climbing the ladder	93
13	Terry at leisure	109
14	And Finally!	115

Chapter 1

Me and how it was

"Bonjour."
Life can lead us into times of adventure and romance, with a touch of fear mixed in. If it hadn't been for events in the 15th and 16th centuries, this book would have been written in French, as the ancestors of the Basson family were Huguenots, being Protestants who were persecuted for their religious beliefs. It is thought that maybe their name came from a Flemish/German mix of 'Huis Genooten', which roughly translated means 'house people', referring to them as a people who studied the bible in secret. They were skilled professionals, artisans and craftsmen and the loss to France became the gain of their new host countries. Many settled in South Africa, Europe and even some as far away as the USA. This exodus was how my ancestors came to England and I have records to show my grandfather, Jacob, living in Thame in Oxfordshire. I have travelled many times through France and I have always felt welcome, almost 'at home', and I often wondered why, when reserving a restaurant table I have never had to spell my name to complete the booking. Today, Basson is a common name in South Africa but, up to only two years ago, the only Bassons I had met were from my close family. However, to my great surprise and delight I found a Norman Basson, in my golf club (Seniors Captain 2011)

and we are hoping, one day, to find a link between our families.

If I had been a child in France, my story would have been one of occupation. My English birthright provided a story about England, fighting a tyranny with little more than bravery and endurance. British wartime kids grew up to honour those who fought to set Europe free.

I am the youngest of three , my brother Arthur being nine years older and my sister Gwen, ten . Yes, I was the baby of the family. I think my parents had given up any idea of having any more children after their second child was born.

Life was very difficult for working class people in those days, so when I arrived in my mother's womb, some ten years after my brother, it was something of a shock and disappointment to her. Mother tried everything to terminate the pregnancy. She did the usual things to bring this unwanted situation to an end. When I did eventually arrive, it was to a mother, who was, to say the least, not overkeen on my arrival.

I remember my Mother telling me, many years later, that she never even had a cot ready for her new little bundle, so a large bottom drawer of the old chest of drawers was hurriedly lined out and made comfy for her unwanted third child. My Father, on the other hand was delighted! He told me many years later that he was somewhat surprised to see his latest child staring up from the drawer chest, with wide open blue eyes, at the light in the centre of the room.

He said he was very proud of his new baby. At six months I had snow white curly hair, and when I was 6 years old he would get my Mother to dress me up and then take me out on his coal round, showing me off to his customers.

Dad was a coal merchant's hawker plying his trade by

Me and how it was

horse and cart around the streets of London. Dad loved his horses; he never drove them too hard. When the last bag of coal was delivered, they knew by the lightening load that their working day was near an end. Their senses became acute, hearing perhaps something of relief in my father's voice when he turned them towards home,

"Get on home then!"

In that sudden moment they sprang to life and Dad would quickly gather up the loose leather reins to gain control, as their hooves struck the cobbled street with a loud clatter. The horses were stabled under the railway arches of Stratford, West Ham. They looked altogether different with their harnesses removed, revealing great steaming bodies and with constant flicks of their heads as they pulled at their net of hay. I was always a little afraid of them, yet my Father assured me they were just gentle giants.

My Father was the youngest of ten. This large family would suggest that we have a great many relations out there, but, sadly my immediate family seemed to have had little interest in keeping in touch with relatives. My paternal grandfather, Jacob, was born in Thame Oxfordshire, of true country stock. He was, by all accounts, a bit of a tyrant to my grandmother, yet in his later life having sowed his wild oats in many a field, he and Grandma in their dotage became very close again. Under this new regime, my Dad said his father would always be home promptly, from the pub, for Sunday lunch. The pub was a ritual meeting place for him and his sons. Yet in days gone past he would hang around the pub until Sunday lunch was spoilt, leaving Lydia very unhappy. My grandfather Jacob died in the arms of my Father, still clinging to life refusing to give it up. He passed away sweating in his fight.

My grandmother, I am told, was a very gentle lady

Romance without kisses

whose only outing was a yearly visit to The Derby with a large family hamper, prepared by her hands alone and with the best horse in the stable and a gig made ready, off they would canter in grand style: Jacob, held a long thin whip cast under the horse's belly, which helped them to pass his neighbours' horses. There was no real open competition, I am told, but a pleasant rivalry existed among his friends about which one had the better high stepping cob. My grandmother always made the most of this single, special annual event. My Father was especially fond of his mother Lydia. It shook his religious convictions, I believe, when his mother died. Both my grandparents are buried in Plashet Road Cemetery, Stratford - Jacob and Lydia Basson.

My Mother Hilda was a strong, sturdy woman. She was twelve years younger than my Father and was one of four being three sisters and one brother. The boy called Tom died very young. Her Father was German, with the surname of Godwin. I don't recall anything of my maternal grandfather, other than he worked for Brooke Bond Tea and he always wore a pin-striped suit and a bowler hat. He also died before I was born, leaving my grandmother with three young girls to rear.

She was a very strong woman and very capable too for she opened up a shop and continued trading while successfully raising her remaining three children, without any assistance from anyone. In fact, the shop was the meeting place of my Mother and Father; he used to make oil deliveries there. My grandmother lived to quite an old age and I remember her very well. In fact, she was the only grandparent still alive when I was born. She also went to Woodbridge with the family during the war years.

I always viewed my Mother as a very hardworking woman who never really made a comfortable home, as you may perceive a home should be. She worked as an Orderly in Whip's Cross Hospital and most of her conversation centred around the Ward Sister, who stalked the wards with great authority. So much did Mother brainwash me into the importance of a Ward Sister that, even today, when I meet a lady of this rank, I find it difficult to get my words out. Mother worked on a Tuberculosis ward for two years. This was when TB was uncontrollable. It was just by chance that a new Sister asked her how long she had been working on the ward. She was shocked when Mother told her the long period over which she had been exposed to this disease.

Mum's resistance to any illness carried her through; she put her job before any other obstacle. Coughs and colds never stopped her; perhaps she was from the seed that made Britain great! She was not a demonstrative person and I cannot remember her giving me a great deal of cuddly love. When I asked her she would pull me close, give me a hug and release me almost as quickly. Neither did she display any great outward affection towards my Dad who, I know, would have loved to have been made a fuss of. But, there you are, you cannot change your nature and perhaps her own upbringing; with her Mother being very busy in her shop few cuddles came towards her. I hope I haven't appeared too harsh on my Mum. I am sure she loved us all in her own way.

My brother, Arthur, was a butcher's boy and worked six days a week until 8 o'clock at night. Times were very hard and I well remember the stories that my Father told of these times, when periods of unemployment occurred it made hardships and hunger bite a bit deeper. It was during one of these periods that Arthur had stolen two eggs from his employer, bringing them home and presenting them to my Father; Dad promptly grabbed the frying pan and heated the fat. It was after cracking the first egg, and not until then, that he gave my brother the most severe telling-off and said that he must never do anything like that ever again!

Arthur was also a great joker. I remember we were all sitting quietly in the living room one Saturday lunchtime when a rap came on the back window. We turned quickly to see who it was and to our shock and horror a pig's head was being held above the stone sill. Only when we heard my brother's insane giggling did we realise what he was up to and we sank back into our chairs with great relief. My Father used to make lovely brawn from a pig's head, pouring the brawn mixture into white earthenware basins to set; it was always considered a great delicacy.

On Sundays, four pints of mussels were served hot in their shells. The mussels had been fed on a special oatmeal mixture for five days, after purchasing them from the barrow that came through the streets. The food was very plain but wholesome. I still fondly remember the great bowls of tripe and onions that my Mother cooked in milk with thickened liquor. Whole onions were skinned and boiled as the vegetable and we would go again and again to the large, cast iron pot on the stove. This kept us warm when we went to bed. Those cold bedrooms I have never forgotten.

My sister, Gwen, was the first to arrive in the family. When she was born she was very small, weighing about 5lbs. Her skin was all shrivelled, said to have been due to my Mother's pregnancy cravings for pickled onions and lemons. I remember my Mother saying that when the midwife first saw Gwen she ordered my Mother to go round to her mother's shop and buy 2lbs of butcher's lard and rub this into Gwen's little body. This was thought to help the parched skin. My sister was born small and remained small. Her two brothers, in their peak, outweighing her by 10 stone. Different as chalk from cheese, but my brother and I (as far as looks were concerned) were carbon copies of each other. Gwen, who had the unfortunate task of looking after me while my Mother was at work, cleaned and looked after the house then took me to meet Mother from work.

I remember how difficult it was to undo my braces, particularly at the back and I would quietly walk to Gwen when I needed to visit the toilet. Without a word, I would turn my back towards her. She instantly knew exactly what to do and would detach the leather straps from the buttons. When I returned I said,

"Do me backs up G'en."

Forty years on, we still remembered and laughed together when I sometimes walked in from the bathroom and said, "Do me backs up G'en."

Chapter 2

The skies over London in 1939

I arrived home from school to find my family huddled around our large Cossa radio listening to the news.

"We are at war with Germany," my father announced!

I wanted my tea and couldn't understand what all this fuss was about, so this information, useless to my childhood ears, drifted almost completely forgotten, until one day the street became full of piles of corrugated iron heaped before each home. My father explained that we had to get this pile of iron into our back garden, which was no mean feat because we lived in a terraced house and so every bit of the iron had to be carried through our home.

Dad and my brother studied the plans that came with the pack.

"What's this all about," I asked.
My brother Arthur replied,

"We are going to build an Air Raid shelter in the back garden. It is called The Anderson Shelter".

First, a big hole was dug into the flowerbed near our back door, then the shelter had to be sunk by a third (about a metre deep). Then the sheets of steel were bolted together. The set aside earth, which had come from digging this great big hole, was finally thrown over the roof of the shelter and patted tightly down. The whole project looked like a giant molehill when we had finished.

"What fun," I said to myself, "another den to play in!"

I had nearly forgotten all about the war. The shelter had vegetables growing in the earth piled on top of it. Dad gave us all instructions that, should he be at work and we hear the air raid siren warning us that bombs were on the way, we were to rush out into our garden shelter, even in the middle of the night!

My Dad joined the ARP (Air Raid Precaution). His job was to run to the aid of those in need during an air raid. Dad had fought in France, in the Somme during World War One so his fear was well under control. While others ran wild with fear during bombing, he just stared up at the skies outside our shelter. This confidence was held by all of us in the Basson family shelter. My Dad was on guard so nothing would harm us.

To a five year old, the war was actually exciting when dashing down the shelter at night; lighting candles in the deep dark earth seemed magical. It was very cold and damp when leaving a warm bed at night. The Anderson Shelter did not have any means of heating, but Dad once again came to the rescue. Many candles were lit and over some of them he placed an upturned flowerpot. The candle stayed alight because of the hole in the bottom of the flowerpot providing air. Heat then transferred itself to the earthenware flowerpot, which nicely returned warmth to our cold hands and bodies. No doubt Dad had brought this heating knowledge back from the trenches of the Somme. Even today, in 2011, I wish I could thank my father for everything he meant to me. Sadly, he died when I was just twenty years old, a time of life when a young man has other unimportant yet engaging things on his mind. I missed that opportunity to really appreciate his love and service to us all. I do so hope I shall, one day, be granted a second opportunity.

After each air raid we carried on as usual with our lives. I never ever realised that the overnight raids meant death to hundreds in London, simply sweeping peoples lives away and destroying families forever. I left for school as usual, yet now the streets had bits of burnt iron called shrapnel scattered all over the place. Children collected the more colourful bits and built up collections of the finest examples. Much like a marble collection, we swapped them according to our taste. These bits of shrapnel were from British shells bursting in the skies, whilst trying to shoot down the German bombers.

Air raids also brought laughter. Our neighbours had gone to live in an area less affected by the bombs so they said we could, during their absence, use their shelter. Dad removed some planking in the garden fence so we could get to the neighbours' side quickly. One night my (maternal) grandmother had made a huge pot of porridge for us all to enjoy. Normally she occupied the shelter in our garden when the Air Raid Siren sounded. We all ran towards the shelters, some of us going through the fence, others in our shelter. Suddenly a cry of fear sounded from my Grandmother, who had decided to distribute the pot of porridge between the occupants of both shelters. Dad rushed out to find Nan Nan (as we called her) stuck in the fence, unable to move, holding the hot pot aloft. Dad hurriedly scrambled past us into the shelter to find his hammer, whilst bombs were dropping all around us. He frantically removed two more fence boards to set Grandma free from her frightening trapped situation. It was a tricky moment amidst laughter and fear. I shall never forget our chuckles!

We continued to live under these threatened skies, which brought death to many of our neighbours and friends. All this was beginning to take its toll on my parents. My father had communicated all this to a lady friend of the family, who lived in Suffolk. We called her Aunt Lil and to this day I have never found out if she was a blood relative of ours. My judgement is probably not. Aunt Lil replied to my father's letters by saying,

"Why not move the family into the country where I live?"

It was a Suffolk town called Woodbridge. My father asked about accommodation in her area.

"Well next door to me is empty, so why not write to the Suffolk local authorities and see if you can become a tenant?" she replied.

Dad did as she advised. He found out that if he obtained work nearby, then the council would consider a tenancy based upon housing someone who worked in the area. Dad found work was obtainable fortifying the beaches against invasion. He applied and got the job. All things then fell into place and action to move us from the dangers of the bombs began. My parents still had issues to resolve like finding work for everyone but after another night of very severe bombing, they were convinced these just had to be overcome!

OUR ANDERSON SHELTER

Chapter 3

We moved and Dad joined up

We moved from London to Woodbridge Suffolk on the 11th December 1941, my brother Arthur's birthday. Poor Arthur, his birthday passed unnoticed that year. We arrived at 46 Edwin Avenue. It was a cold day and my mother cried on our arrival as she hated the country she complained, "So you want to bury me here in the sticks?"

These remarks continued until the log fire was lit and a cuppa brewed. The unpacking went without a hitch, for we had the essentials fast to hand like the kettle, teapot, milk and bread. Edwin Avenue stood on a council estate just on the borders of the old town of Woodbridge. Locals would refer to it as the new town with just a string of shops and a post office. This estate stood close by the A12 and the Sand Pits, which served as a quick route to walk to the town, known as the 'back way'.

Dad took up his new job fortifying the beaches, whilst my mother and sister Gwen looked for local work in the town. This came very quickly for both of them finding jobs in the local Canning Factory. My mother eventually adjusted to the situation, mostly because her family was no longer threatened from bombs dropping out of the skies in London. Dad arrived home after his first day at work, very tired indeed, with stories to tell about how his work was progressing, as they were digging in tank traps on the beaches to defend England from invasion. Clearly this was very hard physical work, yet he was making the best of it with never a moan. An army truck picked him up each day along with about ten other men from the town. He was dropped off again at the bottom of Pytches Road to walk the last mile home. One day as he walked along this road home he noticed a sign stuck on the gates of an army camp. It read,

WANTED
Washers up in our NAAFI canteen

This stopped Dad in his tracks, so in he went and signed up. He felt this position was far nearer home; it must also be better than working so exposed on a cold, windy beach in December. My Dad was always looking to improve himself. Washing up dirty dishes all day was never one of his choice pastimes, so he kept his weather eye open, as they say, for jobs being advertised on the notice board. One day his manager spotted him checking the job market opportunities and asked him if he had ever considered training to become NAAFI manager. Dad grabbed at this chance to improve himself. So leaving behind the kitchen pans, he was sent for training and finally emerged, as a fully-fledged manager.

He was offered his first position as manager of a NAAFI near Woodbridge, which stood no more than three miles from Edwin Avenue. Dad needed to recruit staff, so Mum and Gwen left the Canning Factory to join Dad in this new adventure and Aunt Lil came too. This canteen, on the boundaries of the old town of Woodbridge, was situated within the grounds of a large Elizabethan home called Seckford Hall, which is considered amongst the

We moved and Dad joined up

finest examples of this period. The British army had taken over the hall as their headquarters. His wooden canteen hut had been hurriedly built to serve the troops awaiting embarkation in the grounds some 300 yards from the great home itself, overlooking the A12. The single storey wooden building was very long and built on tall brick piers, standing two feet above the ground. My father walked the three miles from Edwin Avenue each day to and from work.

We just had to have chickens in the garden of our new home in Edwin Avenue. It was wartime and eggs were rationed. We built the chicken hut from scraps of throwaway wood. Having built the shed and run we wanted some fowls to put in them. Dad, on this occasion, thought it would be great to rear some day-old chicks. He therefore acquired a fat broody hen and set her on some dummy chalk eggs. Off we went to our local hatchery, where we wanted all our day old chicks to be ready sexed females!

The hatchery manager agreed to sell us a dozen day-olds and so produced a 12 x12 inch square cardboard box, which had a stiff ring of cardboard inside, to stop the baby chicks from being squeezed into any of the corners and to prevent killing them before we had got them home. Inside the cardboard ring, soft meadow hay was placed on the floor of the box. All this detail was to keep the chicks warm and alive during our journey home.

Proudly we started to walk from the hatchery when I noticed a pile of broken shells set beside the farm gate. We could just make out, "Cheep Cheep!"
The chicks were trying to emerge from this heap of broken shells. These cheeps came from baby chicks unable to get out of those prison like -shells. The hatchery manager had discarded them and considered them to be

Romance without kisses

far below his hatchery standard. It was thought that if a chick could not make its own way out of the shell and into the world it would not be worthwhile keeping it. With some careful picking at the shells we helped six little mites into this world. Dad placed each newborn into his greatcoat pockets, with three in each, to keep them warm. We started again towards home walking tall, for now we had 18 chicks! On our arrival home I wanted to place all our chicks under mother hen straight away, but Dad advised me to wait until dark because she probably would only accept them if she could not see what was happening.

I was very impatient, but Dad insisted that his way was the best course to take. He had raised chickens all his life. As darkness fell we crept out to the shed with the chicks in their box, Dad placed the first chick under the hen by holding it in his almost closed hand to protect it from a peck from mum, who was not sure if she really wanted them. We waited patiently in the dark for a few moments, when suddenly a satisfied deep "cluck" came from the broody hen; this was just what Dad had been waiting to hear. He then placed all the chicks under her. We crept away relieved that we had discharged all of our responsibility for our little ones. I went to bed that night and dreamed of what the future held for our chicks. I slept deeply, satisfied that this day would remain with me for the rest of my life.

The chicks grew well, almost to maturity, which is what is called, 'Point Of Lay'. Dad said it was now time to find them larger quarters. His plan, which had always been in his mind, was to use that large gap under his NAAFI shed at Seckford Hall. Dad came up with the idea of acquiring a roll of camouflaged wire netting from the army barracks. The trouble was it had multi-coloured feathers stuck all over its surface. Resourceful as ever,

We moved and Dad joined up

Dad threw the whole roll of camouflaged netting onto a bonfire and 'Hey Presto!' We had a clean roll of chicken wire. He then surrounded the gap under the hut with this bright wire and the chicken enclosure was made.

Our next problem was how to transport all our chickens the three miles from Edwin Avenue to their new location, under the NAAFI hut at Seckford Hall. This proved an adventure all of its own. We never owned any transport and even if we had owned a car, petrol was almost unobtainable during the war years. This problem was overcome by a three mile round trip, carrying half of our stock in a big tea chest with a handle across the top, walking the main A12 road. We were exhausted, for it had taken up our whole day and a massive amount of energy. During the second journey, we rested under a row of silver birch trees. (They still grow there to this day, a little taller now in 2011). As we sat recovering, I caught sight of a whopping great mushroom, bigger than I had ever seen before! As big as a dinner plate it was. On arriving at his canteen kitchen, Dad immediately set to work frying the huge fungi for our tea. Our chickens thrived and produced many wonderful wartime eggs. The troops used to throw them stale, wartime, yellow cake. They admired our enterprise and, at times, some of our spare eggs.

All that is now left of the old wooden hut is just a scar in the good Suffolk sandy earth, where my wartime childhood memories remain so vivid. I often return to this place sitting happily among the ghosts of my family, thinking, "Gosh what a wonderful period of my young life the Second World War really was."

Seckford Hall is now a 4-star hotel and a great treat for me is to stay there along with family and friends and with my many happy memories.

Chapter 4

Pop's Café

Woodbridge was where the Americans from the 493rd Bomber Squadron visited from their air base in Debach. I well recall their sudden appearance in the town; they were the young men in uniform from whom we kids cadged gum chum. Actually they were almost like aliens descending on a town, steeped in history, that had never seen the likes of these fresh faced young men before.

The Americans were actually a breath of fresh air; the town took to these invaders like cream over strawberries. How exciting it was to be greeted with a smile and casual happy behaviour. I am not suggesting that Suffolk local folk are bereft of these qualities, but the difference was that the GIs smiled and talked to perfect strangers!
It has often been said, "You have to be been born here, to become accepted!"

America had come to help us fight against an evil war going on in mainland Europe, so it was very encouraging to have them send their young men and flying machines to help us win the war. The conditions for them at Debach were far from ideal, as the following veteran's account of how it was in 1944 reveals.

Romance without kisses

This quote from B17 US Tail Gunner, Jack Rude in conversation with Archivist John Lovell, can be found on the Helton's Hellcats Website www.493bgdebach.co.uk and from whom permission has been granted for this to be used by Richard Taylor.

"Living conditions during the winter of 44/45 were very harsh. The Nissan huts were not insulated, rough concrete floors, nearly always covered in mud, only one small stove and only one bucket of coke was the daily ration. Usually three enlisted crews, (non commissioned, 15 or 16 men) in each hut. Officers lived on the same site but on the other side of the road. Two tier bunks were the normal with no locker facilities for storing uniforms or personal items. Everything on the floor, always damp and mice enjoyed this haven. The crews who were not on a mission collected the fuel for the stove, but by the time the mission crew returned, it was all gone. Anything that could burn was stolen. To be in bed was the only place to try and keep warm. As the ablution blocks were freezing, no hot water, it was not unheard of to go to London on a 48-hour pass and spend most of the time in the bath – if you could arrange enough coins to keep the meter going. Keeping the same clothes on 'day and night' for 14 days was about the 'social limit'. Best uniforms were cleaned in 'gasoline' so travelling in a train was dangerous if anyone smoked! Life for flyers was tough on both counts – stay in bed or fly missions. An English winter is not ideal, living in a damp hut or being shot at in the sky at 26,000 ft is no option."

Clearly no red carpet came out to greet these young heroes from the United States. Woodbridge Town offered some warm log fires in many fine old pubs, where real Suffolk Ale was served. The Yanks, as they were called, never understood why we drank warm beer. The dreadful cold winter of 1944/45 caused them to huddle inside our pubs during their spells of relaxation, before they were off again over Germany to risk their young lives for our cause. One of their favourite haunts was the 'Gin Shop' (now torn down); it was a pub with a name that suited the establishment very well. It was also my Dad's favourite watering hole. Dad always drank gin because he said, "Drinking gin is the only relief I get from the pain of my stomach ulcer."

The American uniforms were very well tailored and together with their charm they swept the single girls off their feet. Camp dances were often arranged so the town really buzzed with the arrival of so many young men.

The river Deben naturally attracted the airmen. The boat people offered trips up the river and I became one of their scouts around the town. On one occasion, having sold a trip to a GI, I was asked to meet him and his girlfriend at The Bull Hotel in the market square. I was to call for them at 3pm to guide them down to the boat, so I arrived on time and gave their names to the receptionist. She replied,

"Oh yes, they are in one of our rooms upstairs."

I knocked on their door and a voice said, "Hold on a minute."

The girlfriend opened the door; she asked me to take a seat whilst she put on her stockings whilst the guy was drinking a whisky. It never occurred to me that this hotel room had just been used for casual sex.

I guided them down to the river to a huge wooden boat that had seemingly been moored for a lifetime in the river mud, near the ancient Tide Mill. The owner of the boat was really a strange old man; I do not think his weather-tanned face had anything to do with over exposure. His complexion was sort of dusty like his clothes wearing the same ones week in week out. The reason he wanted me to sell his trips in the town was because no one, in their right sense, would have ever approached to buy a trip from such as him. This was especially true for those smart young men in their tailored uniforms.

The trip was in his long rowing boat, which he lowered into the water without a word of greeting to his passengers. I often watched the hesitation on their faces as they stepped into the boat, possibly regretting ever buying a ticket from me. The old man was a strong skillful oarsman; he knew the Deben and its dangerous currents very well. The only time he gave me the oars to hold was when he wanted to take a 'pee'. This time he walked past the young couple picking up his bailing tin on the way, heading towards the bow. He took a loud toilet break as if no one was on board! All of our mouths dropped open as if lock-jawed. I think I was the most embarrassed; I had sold the tickets to this young couple for a nice sunny trip up the river, not to experience such behaviour. I think the GIs wrote about our ways and strange customs in their letters home. Goodness knows how they described the boat trip on the river Deben!

Dad noticed a small lock up shop for rent in Cumberland Street, Woodbridge next to Creasy the Butchers. He enquired about the premises and, after taking all things into consideration, he felt that it was about the right time to bring his catering skills into play, on his own behalf. He, therefore, resigned his position as NAAFI manager and gave himself a new title of, 'Café Proprietor'.

"What shall I name this new enterprise?" he said. Eventually turning to mum, saying, "Let's open up and see if a name presents itself."

On the first day of opening we were made to have our cooked breakfast in the virgin café. Dad did not allow Mum to clear away any dirty plates.

"Wait until a few customers venture in Hilda. We do not want them to know they have fallen victim to try out our grub for the first time."

All started swimmingly as a few locals were among the first customers. Then came a young American flyer from Debach. With a casual look around he said, "Do you sell black coffee Pop?"

Deliverance had presented itself! Next day Dad had a sign writer paint, 'Pop's Café' on his shop window.

My mother worked very long hours cooking all the meals for the café. My sister Gwen and Aunt Lil also worked for Dad. Opening all hours caused a near meltdown for my mother. Her hair suffered terribly. She had a forties hairstyle, with two rolls of hair set beside each other over her brow. Up early each morning without a minute to lose, caused her to neglect so much of herself, hardly brushing her hair at all. These rolls became knotted and finally she had to cut the matted balls of hair away. She kept these matted lumps and used them to set under the few hairs she had left in this area. You may find it strange that I should remember this situation so vividly but I was so fascinated at the way she camouflaged that she had hardly any hair to speak of over her forehead!

This hairstyle of mother's can be seen in the only picture I still have of her. Poor Mum. How exhausted she must have been. My childish concern was only that rolls of hair might fall off her head into the soup she was about to serve. Kids have some strange thoughts!

"Behind every successful man is a woman."

My mother fulfilled this quotation very well.

Pop's Café opened seven days a week, until 9pm. Americans took my Dad to their hearts. Pop was the talk of the town. He supported local charities. He became a very successful businessman always helping people less fortunate than himself.

He became very concerned about the young London Evacuees and their families that briefly visited their children far away from home. His hand-painted message on his shop window in wet white chalk, became noticed by a journalist.

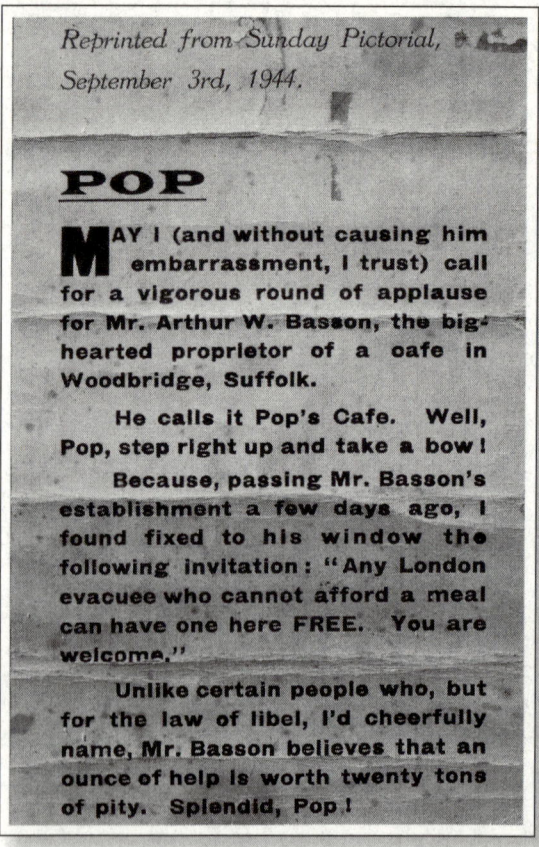

Reprinted from Sunday Pictorial, September 3rd, 1944.

POP

MAY I (and without causing him embarrassment, I trust) call for a vigorous round of applause for Mr. Arthur W. Basson, the big-hearted proprietor of a cafe in Woodbridge, Suffolk.

He calls it Pop's Cafe. Well, Pop, step right up and take a bow!

Because, passing Mr. Basson's establishment a few days ago, I found fixed to his window the following invitation: "Any London evacuee who cannot afford a meal can have one here FREE. You are welcome."

Unlike certain people who, but for the law of libel, I'd cheerfully name, Mr. Basson believes that an ounce of help is worth twenty tons of pity. Splendid, Pop!

Another of Dad's charitable exploits was to invite all the evacuee children, in Woodbridge and surrounding villages, to a visit to the Saturday morning picture house down near the railway station. Dad provisionally booked four rows of seats at the cinema.

He hired a Brass Band to march down Quay Street beginning outside Pop's Cafe. I recall about fifty children turned up with Dad leading the band. Dad had faith in his conviction, but he admitted to me years later, he was so nervous that he had visited the 'Gin Shop' before firing the starter's gun!

The American aircrews asked Pop if he could serve them with hamburgers. Mum had no idea how to make them, nor for that matter, what they looked like. Dad jumped on his bike and cycled to Debach where the 493rd bomber group was based. The guard, who recognised him as the café owner from Woodbridge, stopped him. He explained his plight and a sergeant took him to the camp chef, who not only told him how to make hamburgers but also threw Dad's bike into the back of his jeep and drove him back to Pop's Café, to show Mum how to make and cook them. Entente Cordiale!

It was the Woodbridge kids custom to walk up to an American in uniform and ask, "Have you got any gum chum?"

The stock reply came, "Have you got any sisters mister?"

To this I would reply, "Yes I do."

Thus I sold an introduction to my sister for a single stick of gum (smile).

Gwen eventually fell in love with a young American. His name was Sergeant Billy L Mickle. He was from the Helton Hellcats Squadron of B-17 Flying Fortresses. Billy served as a Radio Countermeasures Operator. They married at the tender age of twenty. My father was not too pleased with this marriage idea and was outspoken enough to say to Billy L, "Look, I have cared for my daughter from a little seedling. Now she is about to flower, you want to take her away from us, back to the States."

Romance without kisses

America, to my father and the rest of us for that matter, was like another planet. When Gwen was gone from our lives we thought we would never see her again. My father's missing signature on their wedding certificate, suggests the rift between my Dad and Billy L had not healed by the time of the wedding.

During the day, Billy L disappeared off to fly a mission over Germany, but, to my childish mind he had just left home, as other men do to go to work. But unlike other men who go to work, Billy L returned home with a look of change all over his face. We noticed that he was very quiet and shaken. Gwen would prepare a meal for him. As we passed the pepper and salt to him, he did not have to shake it; his hand already had enough tremor left over from his daily ordeal.

I adored Billy L. I never gave a jot of thought that my sister would one day have to leave us. Billy L taught me how to make ice cream. First we scooped up fresh snow and then we mixed it with vanilla essence and some sugar. "Hey Presto! We had a bowl of ice cream of sorts."

I wanted a bicycle and Billy L provided one from his base camp. It was painted a green army colour. I just loved that bike, until one day when I was waiting outside the Crown Pub, and a Jeep pulled up beside me. Out stepped two American military police.

"Hey son where did you get that bike?"

Before I felt forced to tell them anything, Billy L came out from the pub and said, "Terry, you ride off home and I will talk to these guys."

When he got home that night he said, "Terry, paint that bike black and file off the serial number, stamped into the bike frame."

I was never troubled or stopped again after complying with Billy's instructions. How he managed to sweet-talk his way out of that one I will never know.

Billy L really settled into the Woodbridge town scene with people warming towards his friendly cheerful ways. He was man's man, as the English call a guy who is always first up to the bar, buying a round of drinks and the first to get into conversation with locals who loved to be treated to a free pint. This opening gambit was a winning formula. His departure after the war was the first time I had experienced 'loss'.

Woodbridge after the war was to experience a life without the Yanks and businesses suffered accordingly. It took years to settle back to being simply a country town beside a river with a railroad to London. For me, of course the memory, of my Army Air Force bike from Debach, still carries me back to a town full of energy and high spirits. The only difference now is that my feet can reach the pedals!

Chapter 5

A Child in Woodbridge

How shall I begin to tell you about this place in Suffolk, which made such an impact upon my life? It is an enjoyable task because Woodbridge and my time there still remain alive and fresh inside me, in my everyday thoughts. I could describe it in a haunting fashion but it is really much more than ghosts coming back to visit me.

   The Town, with its river and railway station with rails that carried me several times along its steel track towards London, but always back is firmly fixed in my memory. Woodbridge is a place set firmly in my time warp, always available for me to walk those splendid wartime years during WW2. My inner child still runs in a forest, near to the town, called 'Leek Hills', where beds of watercress grow fresh and clean in tiny fast streams.

   My heart leapt and danced as I bent to collect the conkers and sweet chestnuts, along with thousands of beechnuts that had escaped their great husks, scattering this bounty onto the good earth under the canopy.

"How unfair life is!" I think, "Why can't we stay young to enjoy and wander forever among such times?

Am I glimpsing Heaven here?

Is this what is meant by eternal life?
I have a feeling it will be just as I have described."

Woodbridge town is on the banks of the river Deben where can be found an ancient Tide Mill. I walked this way most days. How vitally important the river is to the town. Trade and commerce came up this river and the town has benefited over centuries and still today. The River Deben has many dangerous currents, which nearly took the lives of my brother Arthur and me, until the hand of my father lifted us safely back into the boat we had hired for the day. My visits to the fishmonger to collect the heads of sea cod were frequent. They stared with marble eyes at my young intentions, as I knotted them into a bunch and lowered them quietly into the filter of the Great Mill itself. I sat with the hope of catching the big crabs that sheltered in the shadows.

Woodbridge Sand Pits also captured my interests. A huge sandy valley, a mile or so long and a hundred yards deep, had been cut into the good Suffolk earth centuries back. It was close to the town and in my time, used by the village people as a short-cut between the boundaries of the town and the council housing estate, where we lived in Edwin Avenue. The Pits fascinated me. Sand Martins drilled many nesting holes deep into the sandy cliff face and bats in hundreds swooped down the whole length of the pit at dusk. I always accompanied my sister Gwen home after we had seen a movie at the town picture house. She was convinced that the bats wanted to grip hold of her hair. She screamed out in horror as they came near her in the moonlight. With her coat pulled over her head, I guided her through this valley of fear. In some macabre way I actually enjoyed her screams. It made me feel bold and important to her. Gwen was the dearest of sisters. She had a certain quietness about her, which is very hard to describe, unless you sat opposite her with your arms at length holding a hank of knitting wool. My thumbs needed to be held high as she quietly rolled to and fro the hank of wool into a knitting ball. I never deserved such a wonderful sister.

The Woodbridge Canning factory was another town wonder, giving much employment to the local population. It produced the most spectacular canned plums and other fruits in season. It stood amongst a few acres with mature plum trees marking its boundaries. The Woodbridge kids loved to pick these dark luscious plums. They seemed they were just there for the taking, as the foreman never once chased us away. Their tinned fruit always carried a descriptive label with mouth-watering, fantastic pictures. Mum usually came home with a few of those colourful tins, standing them up on the open shelves in the kitchen. They decorated an otherwise dull-painted wartime kitchen; the war had taken the colour out of England, but these tins brought hope for a happier future. I can still remember the glow they conjured up in the kitchen candlelight. Picking wild fruits were among the other pastimes for children . By the pound, we sold hips and haws from the hedgerows to the Food Ministry. Blackberries and apples scrumped from a local orchard were all within our accepted daily collections.

The elderberries we ignored, but the wood of the elder was much more treasured than the fruits of the tree. To make our annual Pop Gun, a length of about twelve inches with a dimension of two inches, was cut from a bush. The Elder wood has a natural pithy core, which was easily pushed out with a hot poker. From the Hazel tree we cut a branch sixteen inches long, just thicker than a finger, leaving four inches as nature had grown it, to make the handle. With our penknives we whittled away at the remainder to make a dowel-like round rod, strong enough to push through the length of the wooden

Romance without kisses

barrel. Acorns were then gathered for ammo. The elder served as a barrel and the hazel was the push rod of our homemade gun. One acorn was banged into each end then pushed out through the core of the Elder with a loud POP! Out shot an acorn travelling some great distance. We created the initial thrust by putting the handle into our tummies as a sort of backstop, to thrust the rod through the elderberry section. Every Woodbridge boy had a patch of red skin around his middle area. The fun stopped, of course, after the acorn season ended and a much-treasured Pop Gun slid from each boy's belt, almost without notice.

The School Holidays came nicely at the time of the corn harvest. When the farmer decided to cut his field, the Tom Tom drums sounded around the town.

"Did you know that the top field is going to be cut tomorrow?"

Off we would go, armed with pickaxe handles, to beat or throw at the rabbits as they fled from the field. This became more intense as the machines moved towards the middle, leaving smaller and smaller hiding places for the rabbits. We kids took home many bold stories of how we had killed that day for the home wartime pot. Actually I attended many corn harvests, but a rabbit never raced past me close enough for me to drop my wooden handle and deal it a mighty blow. Truth be told, I was often handed a dead rabbit to take home from a man with a shotgun, who had had a splendid day shooting many rabbits and rats. The custom was to gut the rabbit on the spot, keeping its pelt intact, spreading open its cleaned body with a sharpened stick about four inches long and then tying the legs together. Off I would race towards home, arriving breathless telling Mum and Dad porkies! (Cockney Slang :Porky Pies means Lies.)

Many Woodbridge boys owned an air rifle. Mine

was a Webley. It fired 0.22 lead slugs. Many of us were good shots. We hunted rabbits and shot at any birds that perched within range. I guess this helped me to become a true marksman when I went into the army. As kids we took our air rifles for repair to a gunsmith who walked using one leg and a crutch. He lived on Melton Hill, but we were never asked inside the house. The gunsmith took instructions about the gun at the door, propping himself up against the doorpost as he examined my rifle.

"Come back in a week's time," he would say.

Then, with some difficulty, he reversed down the hall, as he closed the door, leaving me with just a bit of oilystained paper, with a job number written upon it. Gosh, that week without a gun seemed like months. He never let us down though; the repair always came back on time.

When we returned at the end of the week to visit the Gunsmith holding the repair ticket up high, out came the rifle in tiptop condition. I always tested the gun on the way home by just charging the spring and firing it into the air without any ammo. Bang! Out flew nothing other than gun oil. The sight and smell of that old oily gunsmith with his crutch, shuffling along the passage, holding my Webely rifle still walk and talk to me today. As I write these childhood memories, it astounds me that nine-year-olds back in 1942 were permitted to walk about with Air Rifles, Catapults, Acorn Guns and Pea Shooters and not to mention the Lemonade bombs.

We made bombs from lemonade bottles with stoppers that screwed down. From the bicycle store in the High Street we purchased carbide crystals that were sold to power gas lamps. We used these crystals far more effectively! Into a lemonade bottle we dropped three of these crystals into a very small amount of water. Then, screwing down the bottle top tightly, we placed the bottle bomb under anything we wanted to blow up. Bees nests and things like that were amongst our victims. When carbide is mixed with water it produces a gas which, when placed under pressure, causes the bottle to explode into fragments. We were always careful to have taken cover before the pressure in the bottle got to a point of going off BANG! We grinned as the nest of bees flew into the air and bits of flying glass whizzed above our heads. I think we would have made a formidable 'Kids' Army' had our island ever been invaded back in 1940 – 45.

We kept a rabbit in our front garden in Castle Street because our back gardens consisted of just a paved concrete square, which lead directly to the outside bucket loo. The hutch was made from wooden butter boxes, which were highly prized since boxwood could be used to make many things. We named our rabbit 'Lavender' because it had an unusual habit of chewing the hutch, making a bid for freedom to roam in our front garden where a tall hedgerow of lavender grew. 'Lavender Rabbit' ran and jumped high into the air landing on top of the dense hedge of lavender. She chewed her way along the hedgerow until she was full of the stuff, eventually falling from her lofty perch with sweet smelling breath.

Sadly our neighbours complained bitterly about this pesky rabbit. Dad repaired the hole in the rabbit hutch but she chewed another hole overnight. Several times he repaired the hutch but each morning we found Lavender'had escaped again after chewing more holes to make a break for freedom! With this constant complaining from our neighbours, Dad decided to make our Lavender rabbit into a rabbit pie. Dad could kill anything on four legs, but this rabbit had got under his skin. Dad knew a Woodbridge man who like him, normally had few qualms about killing anything. Apparently this man could kill a rabbit very swiftly. This guy always drank in 'The Cross' pub so Dad took the rabbit one night, to the pub. The killer man came in and Dad explained how it seemed silly, but he would rather not be the hand that dispatched this special rabbit in the sack. The man picked up the sack swiftly and strode back out into the street. He was back in a few moments and said,

"Pop, the deed is done!"

Dad put the sack under his bench seat. With some relief in his voice, he ordered another round of drinks. On his way back from the bar, he noticed the sack was moving across the floor. With tears in his eyes Dad picked up the sack and killed the rabbit with one blow behind the ears. He never spoke to that man again. We buried Lavender Rabbit under her favourite bushes in our front garden in Castle Street. We no longer considered making her into a rabbit pie.

My first sweetheart was a girl called Joy Marsh. She lived with her family and sisters in Brooke Street. I often played with her and her two sisters along the river Deben. She had very long hair and was the prettiest girl in the town. I was so proud to call her my girl-friend. Boys in those days thought only of girls as mere kissing lips. We chased them until all of us were exhausted. Our final approach was to try and kiss one. The girls stood rigid with both hands covering their lips. We tried hard to pull one hand free to grab a kiss. Recovering their breath, off they ran again with us in fast pursuit, hell bent on getting both hands removed next time! To this day I am unsure whether I ever managed to kiss Joy.

So this was my first romance. It was a **'Romance, without Kisses'.**

Romance without kisses

Whatever was between us, certainly lasted with me, for many years and came back to haunt me much later on.

How to make a 'Pop Gun'

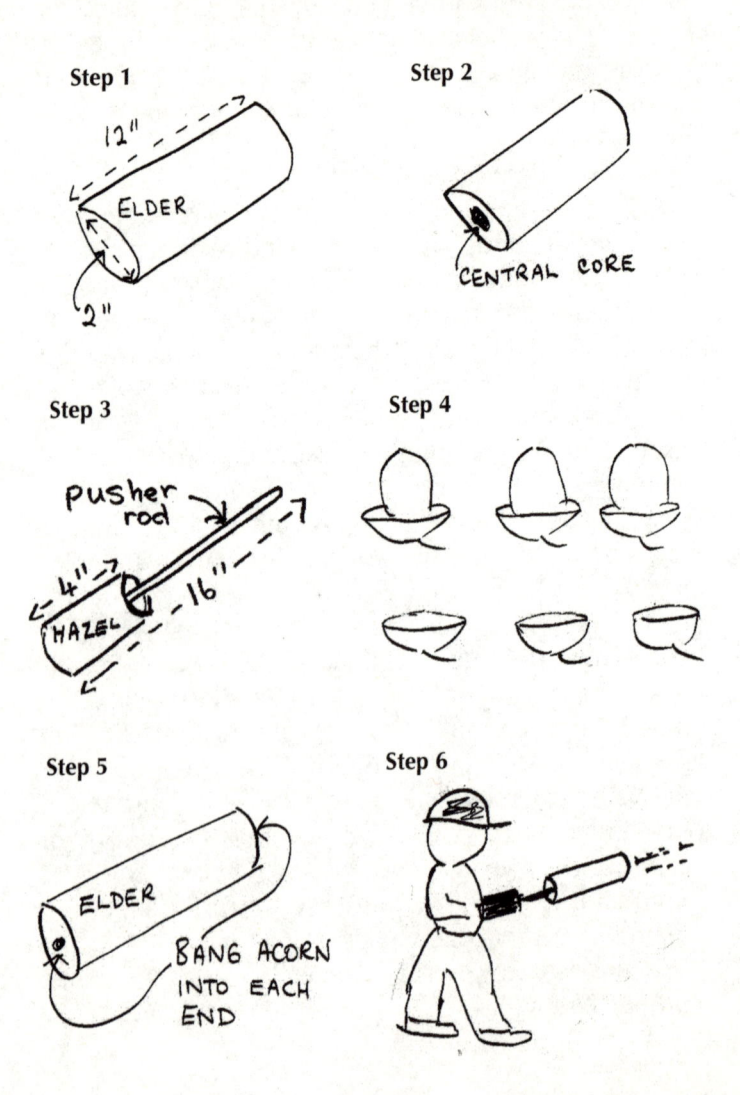

Step 1

12"
ELDER
2"

Step 2

CENTRAL CORE

Step 3

pusher rod
4"
HAZEL
16"

Step 4

Step 5

ELDER
BANG ACORN INTO EACH END

Step 6

Chapter 6

VE Day (Victory in Europe)

The news came to us in Woodbridge amid cheers ringing throughout the World. The BBC broadcast the words of Winston Churchill, "We may allow ourselves a brief period of rejoicing."

The end of the war in Europe did not mean the war with Japan was over, however wartime Woodbridge was over and so were the times that had woven a net of memories in my young mind. We celebrated VE day around Thomas Seckford's Shire Hall at the top of the hill. Hundreds of people gathered with flags flying. Music and song lead to street dancing with the young American aircrews, who were ecstatic. Yet this day was the start of mixed emotions, with goodbyes to young men from the American Army Air Corps. Their girlfriends cried as they waved them back towards their homeland once again. I sat on the steps, in the front of the Shire Hall, and watched the VE celebrations proceed throughout the day and long into the dark hours. I looked down at a statue of Queen Victoria in the churchyard realising that the year she had died was the year my father was born.

Gwen and her son Billy A were also preparing to

go to the USA along with Billy L. Sadly for Gwen, this was not to be until nearly two years after her husband had gone back home. The GI war brides, as they were named, waited far too long before the US government granted the necessary financial aid to pay their passage over. Young Billy was three when I said goodbye to him and my sister. I remember those touching moments very well. Baby Billy was such a dear friend, with whom I had played from his cradle days to toddling, around our home in Castle Street. Dad realised that his magnificent money-making Pop's Café would never be the same again without the American aircrews; it could no longer support the staffing levels. Mum thought it was a good time to restate her original complaint about being buried in the country. This time, Dad could not find a reason for us to stay in Woodbridge, but he waited yet another two years after the war, trying to keep the family together until Gwen and her child left us for America.

Poor Gwen had so many trials to bear in this period of her life which was to change forever. Plans were made to gather all the GI brides and their babies together to sail on a troop ship from Southampton. She arrived ahead of many others so was forced to wait for all to be assembled. This was a dreadful experience as conditions were cramped, dirty and so unsettling that the babies were crying too, having picked up their mothers' anxieties. She put up with these conditions for three days but there was never any announcement or update on when the boat would be ready to sail. In desperation, she asked to leave the ship but this was refused. She was so distraught that she approached the captain with the same request saying that, if he refused, she would be forced to throw herself and her child overboard. He had no alternative but to agree. Dad came to the rescue by bringing her back home and with yet another sad goodbye she left

VE Day (Victory in Europe)

once more but this time flying to America on a ticket paid by a father, who really couldn't afford the cost at that time. It was two years after Pop's Café had been closed and funds were dwindling.

The two-year gap from war ending to Gwen's departure was much like the Curate's egg (good in parts). Pop's Café changed to keeping normal hours which meant my Mum and Dad came home much earlier. Sadly they still retained the habit of going out to the pub most nights, leaving me after tea, to find my own enjoyment. If my brother was alive today and reading this, he would realise that it was not all sweetness and light, when he always thought that I had experienced the best time of our family's life. Yes, we were richer but Arthur and Gwen had more family unity, with evenings around the radio rather than 'down the pub'. I always knew how to find them, peering into the pub door after dark calling out to Mum and Dad. One of them would come out and say, "Hello Terry would you like a lemonade?"

Half an hour passed, when again they appeared holding a packet of crisps.

"Are you going to be long Dad?" I would ask.

This was repeated over and over again, with me bursting with lemonade and stuffed with crisps. I sat out on the empty crates until finally they came out to walk home, after the pub landlord had rung last orders several times. This was not the only bad news because they argued all the way home. Their marriage was not made in heaven, for me these times were more like hell; it was so exhausting as the rows between my Dad and Mum greatly affected me. Even today my stomach turns when disputes occur in my life. During times like this, I find myself moving as far away as possible from tension. With the war over Pops Café became just another of the tearooms in the town.

Chapter 7

Return to London

It was a sad day for me when Dad arranged for us to return to London, now that the American army aircrews had all gone home after the war.

"There is little business to be had from just the townsfolk," he said.

I well remember that eventful day as we packed up all our goods and chattels onto the removal lorry. We left the large sofa last to put on the tailgate, to give us a seat for the journey. Yes, we all travelled back to London on the same lorry that was moving all our bits and pieces. I watched from the travelling sofa with tears running down my cheeks as Suffolk disappeared from our view. I eventually fell asleep and when I awoke the greenness had all disappeared to be replaced by rows of grey drab houses, around the Royal Albert Dock in Custom House, West Ham.

Leyes Road was our destination. It was a vacant shop next door to Meyes the German bakers. Pop's Café, number two, was opened to serve the dockworkers from the Albert Dock. They proved to be a very different clientèle from the GI airmen back in Woodbridge. I hated the place; gone were the green fields and the

Romance without kisses

open places like the sandpits, where I had so many adventures. Replacing them were just rows of Edwardian houses with a Gas Works on the horizon. The people in this area were attempting to recover from the war. The Albert Dock had received much attention from the German bombing raids, which were trying to hit the docks to cripple Britain's incoming vital supplies. At this time my brother Arthur arrived home demobbed from the Marines. He started work in the café until he said to Dad one day, as Dad was making his way up the stairs to have an afternoon nap, "Dad, when is it my turn for a kip?"

Dad replied, "I think after that remark Arthur, it is now time for you to go and find yourself another place to work."

My brother found work at the bottom of Leyes road in a yard that sold logs and creosote. He drove the delivery lorry and, when he was not out on the road, he filled hundreds of gallon cans from a vast vat of creosote. The cans had large cork stoppers. After filling say fifty cans, he then proceeded to bang in large cork bungs with a wooden mallet. As he did so, he would shout, "Give it a corker!"

Just writing these words makes me smile as I can, hear his voice so loud and clear again,

"Give it a Co……r……. ker!"

This became a family catch phrase.

Arthur was always on the lookout for a good dog, when one day whilst he stood at a bus stop he got talking with a woman, who had an Alsatian dog on a lead. My brother made a fuss of it by saying how he would like a dog like that one,

"I would part with him for a fiver," she repied.

Arthur took a five pound note out of his pocket and came home with the dog. Some weeks later he sold the dog making a £5 profit. Arthur thought this was a good way of making some money on the side, so he purchased another big German Shepherd very cheaply. He came home with this dog then took him up the to pub in Prince Regents Lane, to show our Dad who was having a pint there. The dog seemed friendly enough as he sat under the bar bench, looking at all the new faces that came into the saloon bar. It was not long before a customer came up to stroke the dog. Without warning, the dog growled and bit this guy on the hand. The man complained bitterly to my brother, saying that Arthur should have warned him that the dog was not to be touched. My Dad calmed the man down, telling him that his son had just bought the dog and they had no idea that the dog would act like that. Dad took control of the situation, picking up the dog's lead and, with a mighty brave tug, he pulled the dog to his feet and off he and my brother toddled back home with the dog, reluctantly, following.

Early next morning, my Mum came downstairs to make a cuppa, forgetting all about the new dog. Oh yes, he flew straight at Mum growling his head off. She hastily shut the door to the stairs and came back up and told Dad all about what had just happened. Dad got out of bed and went downstairs, walked boldly into the sitting room. He was not attacked as Mum had been, but nevertheless he let out a shout for my brother to get up and to come downstairs immediately, to see what his dog had done to the furniture! Overnight this dog had chewed all the soft furniture to shreds. My father ordered my brother to get the dog out of the house and find another home for him. Arthur thought about offering him to Bill Meyes, our baker next door, who was often burgled; he thought that Bill might like to buy himself a good guard dog. He walked into the baker's shop with the dog on a lead.

Romance without kisses

Bill was standing at the counter. Before Arthur had got a word out to introduce the baker to his idea, the dog charged at the baker who frantically retreated further behind the counter, throwing bits of hot Bread Pudding at the dog's mouth to delay the charge.

The baker cried out, "Get that bastard out of my shop, Arthur Basson!"

My brother was stumped, until a thought came into his head. "I know," he said, "I will take him to where I work among the logs and creosote."

So, 'The Bastard', as they later named him, lived and slept at the yard where Arthur worked without too much further trouble. One day Arthur was using the saw bench to cut more logs. The saw made a loud buzzing noise so you couldn't hear yourself talk when it was working. On one occasion my brother noticed that 'The Bastard's' ears had suddenly become pricked and alert. Off the dog went like a shot out of a gun. Arthur stopped the saw and listened. Suddenly he heard a man's cries for help. The Creosote yard was next door to a pig farm where the 'Lings', a notorious family as hard as nails lived. They would slit the throat of a pig and at the same time using the other hand roll a fag. Hard men, yes indeed! Arthur chased after 'The Bastard' and found him pinning one of the Ling brothers against the boundary wall.

"Get this dog off me for God's sake, he intends to kill me!"

The Lings never ever took a shortcut again through Arthur's creosote yard.

Arthur became very friendly with one of the baker's sons next door to Pop's Café no. 2. He went out drinking with Eddie Meyes on occasions. One day in the summer, my brother asked if I would like to go with him to one of the baker's drinking holes. Wow! That was so exciting for me, as it made me feel wanted and a little more grown up. We arrived at the pub which I think was called, 'The Warren Wood' in Epping Forest. We sat in the garden and Arthur said, "Would you like to see the Water Otter Terry?"

"Yes I would," came my swift reply.

We walked around the back of the pub and there was a great big iron tank, with a heavy chain disappearing into the water.

"Oh!" my brother said, "it looks like the Otter has gone to sleep below the water. Never mind, I will wake him up by pulling on this chain."

"No, No, Arthur." I begged him to leave it sleeping.

Arthur, pretending not to hear, pulled very hard on the chain, ignoring my pleas. The chain rattled loudly against the tank. I stood petrified at what would emerge and what would be the Otter's frame of mind when he was yanked to the surface. Suddenly with a great shout from my brother, "Out you come you bugger!"

I closed my eyes out of fear. When I opened them again Arthur had a grin on his face and a large old kettle full of holes in his hands.

"Is this the Water Otter you were scared of meeting Terry?"

When my father received the first communication from Gwen in America, he read the letter out to all of us. She was very unhappy and pregnant again with a second child. She reported that her husband had taken up with other women, but when she challenged him on this he became violent and on one occasion tried to strangle her. Dad was beside himself with worry; he drew out most of his savings and sent a ticket out to her for the first possible flight home from the States. My brother pleaded with him not to bring her home, knowing that Dad's finances were no longer what they once were. Pop's Café number two was not the money-spinner number one had been. Arthur's point was to leave her there to work it out but Dad would have none of it. Drawing his savings out of the bank was not an issue; his daughter needed him and that was that!

We will never know exactly what happened in America, but what we do know is that Dad, being the Dad I loved, always put his family first, even when it was at his own expense. He may not have been right, as it may have been better for her and her son Billy to stay and work it out with Billy L. This was Arthur's point, but we will never know who was correct. What I was made aware of, some fifty years later, was that the real tragedy of this story was that young Billy, at the age of five was abandoned. This was not only by his mother but his father also left his child for his grandparents to raise. Many years later, Gwen's mother-in-law informed her, that Billy had stopped eating after she had left and she thought she would have to contact Gwen, to bring her back. It has taken me years to find answers to this and in truth I always felt guilty for my sister's actions. I can understand, after having seen Wilburton myself, that it was so different from what she was used to, but I cannot understand how she could leave such a young child, unless she was refused the chance to take Billy home. It may have been wishful thinking on her behalf, that she thought Billy L would follow, or she may have 'cooked up' that story for our sakes.

Gwen arrived back in the UK four months pregnant, with a boy child who was later named after me, as Terry Wayne Mickle. When she arrived home we asked about her first child Billy. She explained that her husband intended to follow her back with the boy Billy. He said he liked England so much, enough to come back and spend his life amongst us, but this never happened. I cannot confirm any of the truth about the issues of

Return to London

Gwen's problems in the States. I simply write here what I was told. Gwen and her son Terry remained part of our lives, living with my parents until their deaths. She remained single and unhappy. Gwen worked very hard to raise her son, with financial support from my Father but not from State Welfare either here or abroad. Some years later Terry Wayne finally went to the States to meet his father and his brother.

For me, the family's return to London became very difficult. I started at Ashburton School where the children were unkind to me, as I sounded very foreign to them with my Suffolk accent. The Suffolk dialect had some strange ways of expressing things and so that further alienated me from them. The one thing I did excel at was sports; in the 100-yard sprint I could outrun the best in the school but sadly did not make me any friends. One day a boy came up and called me a country bumpkin and punched me in the stomach. I went home crying to my Dad and pleaded with him to send me back to Woodbridge; this went on for months. I became so upset that Dad decided his country boy would never settle back again in a London school. He still had great friends in Woodbridge, so he arranged for me to return. Going back to my wonderful Woodbridge and staying with Dad's friends, seemed to be exactly what I needed.

Dad booked two train tickets, a single for me and a return ticket for him. On the day of our arrival at Woodbridge station his friends were there to greet us. We stayed overnight with them and early the next day, Dad took me to see the Head-Master and explained how I had never settled and was bullied constantly so the headmaster agreed for me to return to my old class. Everything that I wanted was now available. Dad's return ticket was for the one o'clock train; we walked down Quay Street towards the station hand in hand; we had just passed the 'Cross pub', when the whole situation hit me. Sure, I had got my Woodbridge back but it had meant that I had to say goodbye to my Dad who had given me everything I had asked for. Yes indeed, I looked up at him as we walked silently down the hill and said, "Dad, can I come home with you?"

He never said a word. He just gripped my hand a little tighter and we both broke into a trot to catch the train home. I have no idea how he undid all the arrangements, but not a word in anger did he ever level at me. Perhaps he always hoped that this would be the outcome. A father in a million was Mr Arthur William Basson. He will be with me always into infinity and beyond! I eventually settled back into a London school life. I won many prizes running my 100-yard dash for the school. As school champion, I was taken by the gym master to White City to see the world record holder for the 100 yard dash. He was Macdonald Bailey and was a black American athlete.

Pop's café number two just about managed to return a living for the Bassons and the family adjusted again to some hard-up times. I still longed to see my sweetheart Joy Marsh again, and I remember asking Dad how long it would take me to pedal my bike back to Woodbridge. Dad explained this would be impossible on a bike. I had no idea how far it was, but my desire to see her again often came to the surface. Dad was now struggling financially and often said he should have had Pop's Café number two first; he then would have realised how profitable number one was. My mother never ever thought back to Woodbridge, but I know my Dad did often.

One day, Dad said, "Terry, fancy a trip to Woodbridge?"

Arthur was also very keen. Arthur wanted to go just for the ride because his love for the place had never developed, as the times of Pop's Café meant little to him.

Return to London

I was so excited with the thought of again meeting up with my sweetheart Joy Marsh after a year's absence. Dad hired a car and off we went towards Suffolk. Some two hours later, I then understood why Dad had stopped me from throwing a leg over my bike, to go see my old girlfriend. Arriving back in the town was a big event for Dad and me. We had arranged to stay with one of Dad's old Woodbridge chums. The car stopped outside the Shire Hall and I was off like a shot to those old haunts, where I thought I would meet Joy and her sisters again. They often played around the station and the river so I climbed the long iron flight of stairs, which formed a bridge over the railway track. I was in luck! Joy was standing on the bridge with her friends. I rushed headlong towards her shouting her name out loudly.

"Joy, Joy!"

When I eventually got face to face she, I think, had completely forgotten me because she seemed a little confused. Perhaps I had embarrassed her in front of her chums? I played with them until it was time to go to find my Dad and brother. Sure enough, as I had guessed, they were in the pub not far from where the car had stopped. Returning to Woodbridge for the second time did not bring what I had dreamt about for over a year. It was my intention to start up a distant friendship and perhaps come back to Woodbridge one day, and marry Joy Marsh. Once again my romance without kisses was haunting me. This thought remained in my head and never actually left me. Her name was to jolt me back into this time zone again many years later. With all this stored away in my head, memories of my childhood fantasies coupled with splendid times, could never disappear. So I grew up around the Dockland area and the streets of London became the accepted norm.

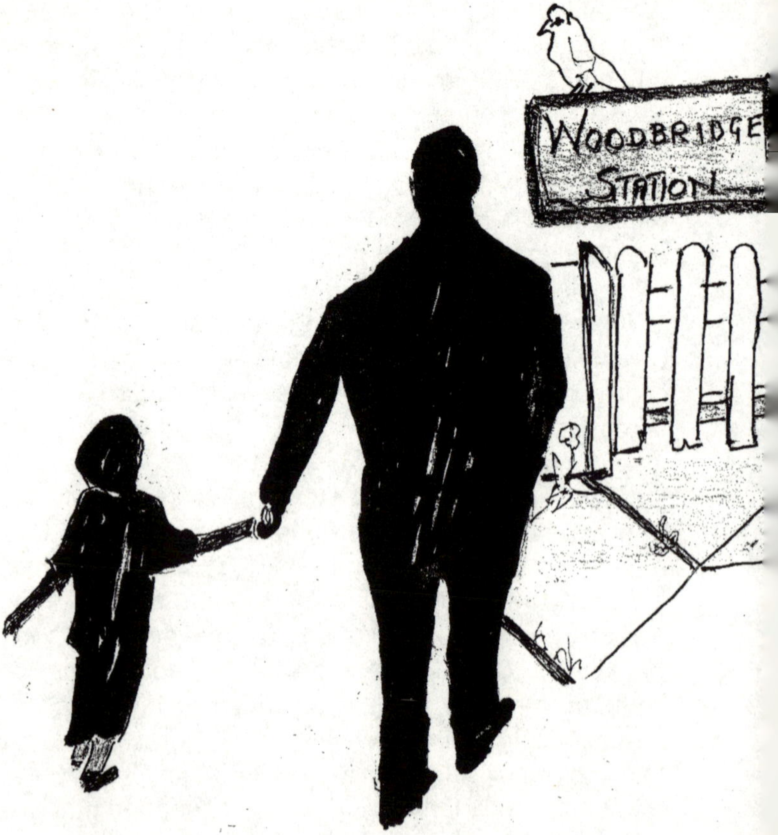
WOODBRIDGE
STATION

Chapter 8

A Yank returns much later on

I married a very attractive Stratford girl from West Ham, meeting her for the first time at the picture house in the Broadway, Stratford. I was on leave from Germany, where I spent two years of my young life doing my National Service. Her Name was Jean Window.

"Easily seen through," she would say to me.

I was demobbed in 1954 starting back to work for a company down in Bow called Wylie, who made safe load indicators for cranes. This work took me away from home, sometimes for a whole week. I had arranged to see Jean Window over the weekend as we really got on very well, but on Monday I was sent to the Steel Company of Wales; I forgot to phone her to say I would be away all that week. When I did return and picked up the phone to her, she began to cry saying,

"I thought you had gone off me and disappeared."

This was the first indication that she really thought a lot about me. The feelings were mutual, but clearly I had never shown my deeper feelings towards her. During our brief courtship, I purchased a 1930 Morris Minor from my brother for £12. He had paid £15. Arthur read that the car was up for sale on a notice board in the local newspaper shop. When he went to see the car, the owner took him and his youngest son out for a spin. My brother had no idea if the car was a good buy. Then suddenly, there was a clang and the owner stopped the car, saying that the starter handle had just fallen off. He jumped out and as quick as a flash my brother turned towards the boy and asked, "Does your father have lots of problems with this car?"

"No it goes fine," the boy replied.

Arthur smiled as he thought that children never lie. So he bought the car when it finally came to rest back at the owner's home. The registration number was UF 5904. We all fondly referred to the car as Little Uff Uff. I hand-painted it a matt black and on the side of the bonnet I painted Jean in white lettering. Jean thought it was real cool.

As I said it was a short courtship; I proposed to her at the age of 21, when she was barely 18. We married in Stratford Church in the centre of the town; she bore me two wonderful boys namely Peter and David. Our lives showed the usual marks of a young couple's struggles to set up a home together. We continued to save until we had enough money to put a deposit down to buy our first home; this took us over six years. Then like all couples we had our share of worry of how to pay the mortgage. Outside of this we were extremely happy bringing up our children.

During all this time Gwen lived with our Mum and Dad in Forest Gate, raising her son Terry as best she could. She never received any financial help from her husband in America. I understand that she did exchange letters with her young son Billy A Mickle and sent some books, like Treasure Island, to him. I was occupied with

Arthur Basson with his
1930 Morris Minor,
'Uf Uf'

Out on Dad's coal cart.
From left to right,
Arthur Basson, Terry
Basson and Dad

POP'S CAFÉ
From left to right, Mum, Aunt Lil, Me and Dad – 1944

Myself in Winchester, age 20, last day in the Army

From Left to right, Derek Ford, John Nash, Fred Grainger (kneeling), Me, Decca

Trebor Sweet Factory, Forest Gate

The Reads'
18 Benhall Green,
Saxmundham, Suffolk

Let's Talk! *Your letters*

Thanks for all the memories – but surely I don't look that old...?

...e memories were recounted in last month's issue.

Just wanted to say, thank you for the way you presented my childhood memories and thanks to Lucy for her pictures! They were so good that the reality of my age was a shock for me. You see, I still feel young inside and have difficulty coming to terms with the ageing process. As an artist, my self portraits enable me to paint the youth I still feel inside and this is something of amusement to my sons!

I have received a call from David Allen he worked as a butcher boy next door to Pop's Cafe and he clearly remembers my mother and father. I am going to meet up with him in the coming weeks.

I am holding my breath in the hope Joy Marsh of Brook Street gets in contact. You never forget your first sweetheart!

TERRY BASSON
Station Cottages
Wakes Colne
Essex

■ Are you still young at heart, but like Terry get a shock when you look in the mirror? Tell us your story.

Your letters come from far and wid...

'Let's Talk' Magazine, letters section

(Inset) The Marsh sisters in 1944
From Left to right, Janet, Aunt Milly, Joy, Shirley, Girly the dog and Tibbles the cat

Birth place of Billy A. – Castle Street, Woodbridge

At Seckford Hall – Before we dined

Fish 'n' Chips – 'The Ship', Dunwich

Meeting after the bomb scare – The George Hotel, Colchester
From left to right, Terry Basson, Carly Basson, Alan Basson, Billy A Mickle

Saying farewell at Heathrow Airport
(top row) Kate Basson, Gaby Basson, Fran Mickle
(bottom row) Terry Basson, Billy A, Isobel Basson and my late son Peter.

Reprinted from Sunday Pictorial, September 3rd, 1944.

POP

MAY I (and without causing him embarrassment, I trust) call for a vigorous round of applause for Mr. Arthur W. Basson, the big-hearted proprietor of a cafe in Woodbridge, Suffolk.

He calls it Pop's Cafe. Well, Pop, step right up and take a bow!

Because, passing Mr. Basson's establishment a few days ago, I found fixed to his window the following invitation: "Any London evacuee who cannot afford a meal can have one here FREE. You are welcome."

Unlike certain people who, but for the law of libel, I'd cheerfully name, Mr. Basson believes that an ounce of help is worth twenty tons of pity. Splendid, Pop!

Reprinted excerpt from the Sunday Pictorial, 1944
(Inset) School photograph of me age 6, 1940

The children of Sergeant Billy. L. Mickle. The two boys in red are my sister, Gwen's, sons.
From Left to right Mike, Billy, Frances, Elizabeth, Terry.

My son, David and Grandchildren, Archie and Saxon in front of the Imperial War Museum, London

The sons of my brother. Bob, Carly and Alan Basson, 1988

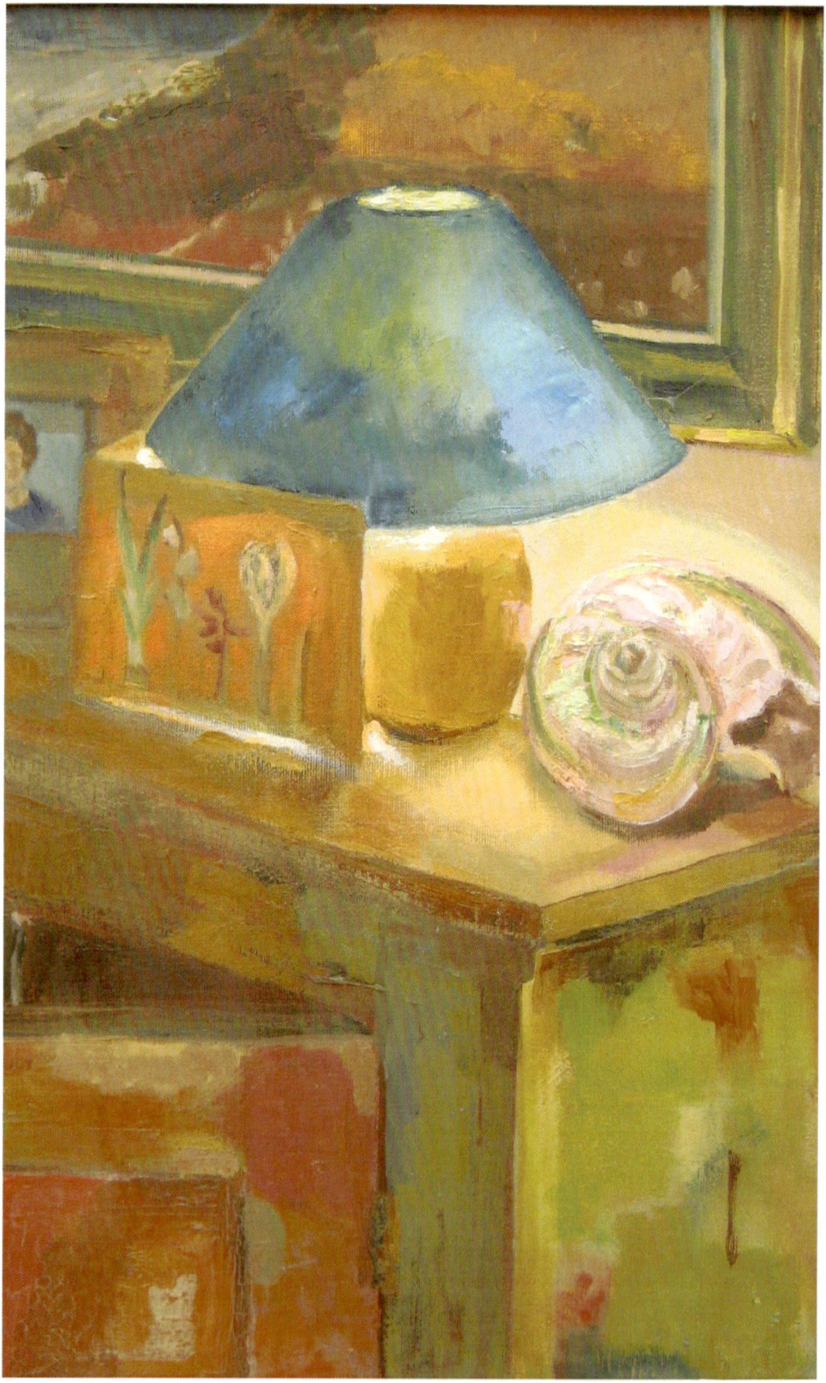

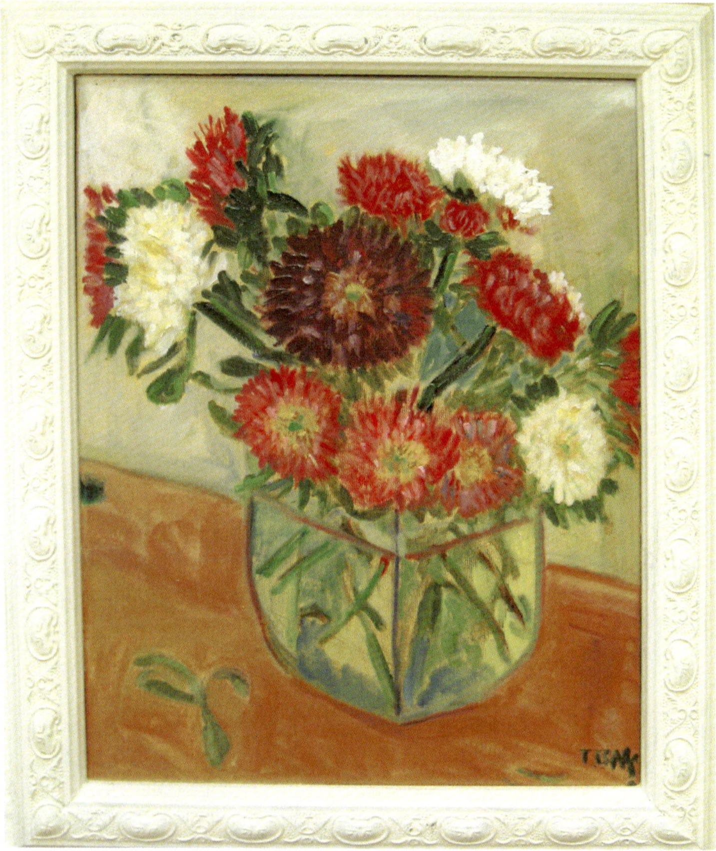

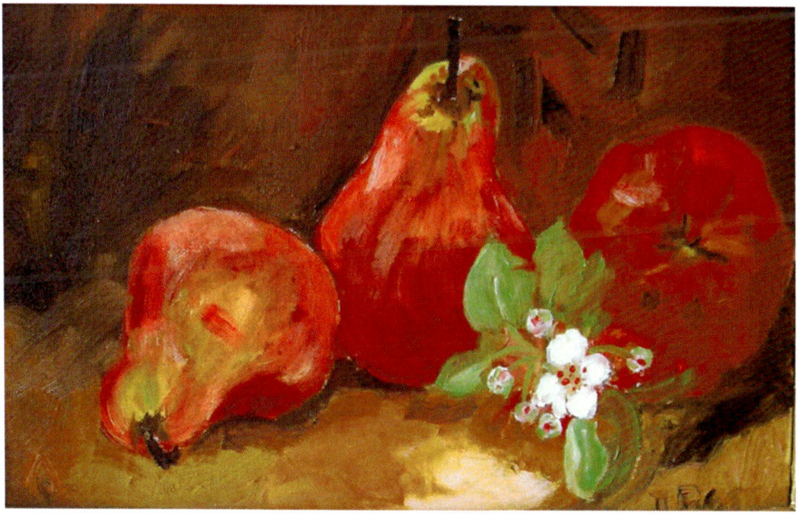

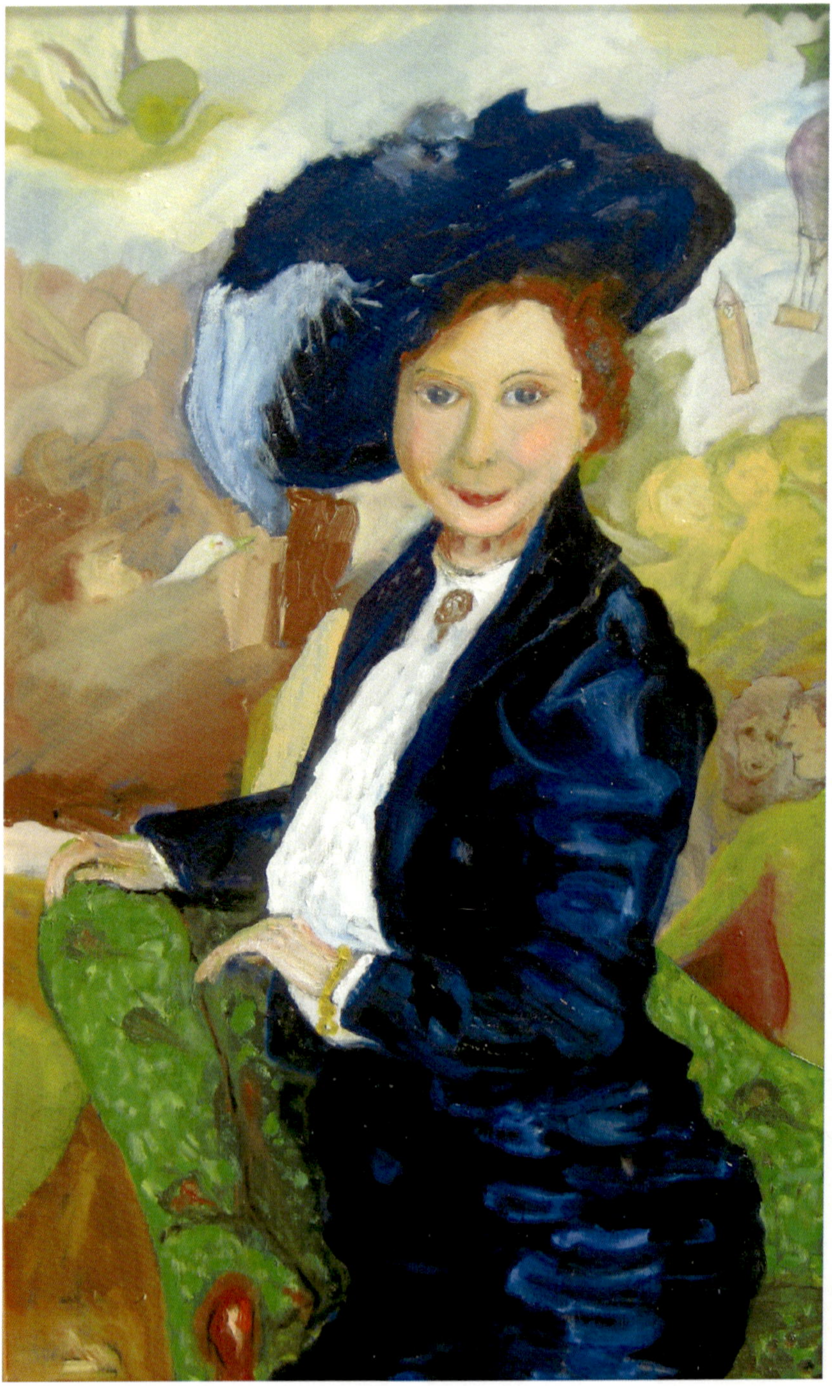

getting a living, being too taken up with my own life to ask her much about her son in America. This being my declared truth, I now feel very ashamed of myself for not engaging with her more about her struggles to make a living. I know she had two jobs with evening work thrown in. I recall many years later when Gwen came over to our home in Shakespeare Road, Walthamstow for Sunday tea. She and mum were often invited by Jean to spend time with us over the weekend. The phone rang and I found myself talking to an American voice asking for Gwen. I handed the phone over to her. When the conversation was over she dropped onto the sofa and cried out loud, "My husband Bill is dead,"

The father of her son Billy, who had deserted them both, had died. I could not get my head around this outpouring of sadness. After all, he had divorced her and had never supported his English younger son Terry. Yet here was my sister crying after her late husband Sgt. Billy L Mickle.

After our father and mother died, Gwen fell into a deep depression. Whilst under this mental trauma, she accepted an invitation from her husband's brother to go to live in America. I guess she wanted to try to recapture some of the lost years with her son Billy. She gave notice to her housing authority and off she flew. I begged her not to leave us, but she was so determined to go back to where she, perhaps, always regretted leaving. She was only 59 at the time, without a state pension and little or no money in the bank. When she arrived in the States, I guess all her American kin were shocked to find that she needed total support. I understand a home was found for her and her food was also provided. Gwen had become welfare dependent many years before Mum finally died. So her mindset was not, 'How shall I finance myself in America?' This was all provided here in the UK by welfare handouts. Her dependency culture must have been a great shock to our American family, who had no idea about her finances when they invited her over. One does make such invitations without thinking too much about the financial aspect.

"Come over Gwen and live with us," was perhaps, just a casual remark that she later accepted.

After only six weeks in America she was back on my doorstep. Her state of mind could only be described as completely broken, without a home to live in or a stick of furniture to call her own. Jean and I clubbed together and found a nice flat in the village of Old Harlow in Essex. She lived out her life happily there without any complaints yet she had much to think about the 'why of it all'.

In the last week of her life I visited her in her home just a week before Christmas. I took her a Poinsettia plant in its Christmas red glow. She said, "Terry I feel I need someone to cuddle me."

I picked her up bodily and provided what she had asked for. I thank God that I was there for my dear sister at the right time, for her end was nearly there. She died in Harlow General Hospital a few weeks later. My brother's son Alan phoned me to say she was very sick and to get to the hospital as quickly as I could; I was living in London at that time. When I arrived at Harlow station Alan was standing beside his car waiting near the station entrance. One look at him was enough to tell me I was too late. I had now lost all of my siblings and a great deal of my personal life had become a deep struggle.

Many years later, I was in France on Omaha Beach when I decided to visit the American War Cemetery. I got into discussion with a coach load of visiting American lawyers and I told them that I was hunting the whereabouts of my lost nephew, who I thought might

have been involved within the legal profession. One guy off the coach seemed very interested and took my details. Sadly nothing came of this enquiry, so I was at the point of giving up, when a little voice inside me said, "Try again for Gwen's sake."
Later at home I sat alone in front of my computer. Again I was prodded by a voice inside me saying, "Try and locate the whereabouts of Gwen's young Billy."

Yet young Billy, I am sure, had no idea about me or my family or my brother's family, which together amounted to one uncle and five full cousins. I looked on the websites for missing relatives. I filled out the questionnaire of what little I knew about this missing relative, who had left us in Woodbridge when he was just three years old. With this done, I relaxed thinking I have now done everything possible to find my American nephew. Three days later I received an email from a woman called Trish, who wrote saying, "I think the man you are looking for has his own website."

I hit the keys and up popped a factsheet with a picture. I looked at it closely and a part of my sister smiled back at me. Sure enough, I had found my American nephew who had become a Senator of Oklahoma. I was so excited about finding my lost sister's son after a gap of some 56 years, so I sat down to write to him and introduce myself.

"Gosh," I thought, "how and what should I say?"

I started by explaining who I was, and added that if perhaps he did not want to reply, I would understand how he might be feeling after being abandoned by his English mother. After all he might have been resentful towards the English side of him. It was a very difficult letter to write. I was hoping for it to bring some light into both of our lives and yet I was prepared for the worst.

Billy's answer was as positive as a sunny day after

a week of dreadful weather. It turned out he was very proud of the half-English side of his make-up and no, he held no grudges. With all this news singing in my ears we corresponded regularly and I got to know him a little better. I then received an email from him, saying he would like to come over and spend a week here with his wife, Fran. This news came at the time when my second wife had left me to live on her own. So the prospect of this visit meant I had to entertain them alone. I dreaded being a single host, but was determined to greet them with open arms and make best of the situation.

Billy asked me to find him accommodation for his week's visit. I pre-booked two nights in 'The George', Colchester and the remainder of the week at Seckford Hall Hotel, just outside Woodbridge, where my Dad's NAAFI had been during World War Two. I arranged to meet Billy and Fran under the clock in Liverpool Street Station, a meeting place that Noel Coward had used in many of his romantic stories. Before leaving home to go to the station, I decided to make up some egg and cress sandwiches . I intended to bring my American family back to my single, lonely home for a cup of tea. I arrived at Liverpool Street Station much on time. Standing under the clock as straight as a soldier, I remained like this for over an hour after the arranged time to meet them. I was becoming somewhat anxious, when suddenly my mobile rang and an American voice said, "Where are you Terry?"

"Under the clock," I replied.

"Well, we have been standing under a clock for a long time and cannot see you," Billy answered

It turned out that Billy and Fran were under the street clock where they assumed I had meant. This was the old original clock featured in so many of Coward's scripts. Silly me, I was standing under the electric clock on the station platform! With this misunderstanding over, Billy came out of a crowd of people with his hand towards mine. We embraced and hugged. This was a reunion 56 years after we had played together around Pop's Café in Woodbridge Suffolk. My sister's Yank had returned!

I took Billy and Fran home to Wakes Colne where I made them some tea and served the egg and cress sandwiches. After tea, I drove them to 'The George' in Colchester for their first two-night stay. We were within a hundred yards of the hotel, when a policeman walked out in front of the car and waved me over to stop.

"Sorry sir, you cannot go any further into the High Street," said the police officer.

"Why?" I asked.

"We are dealing with a bomb scare," he replied.

I felt so embarrassed to have booked my American family into a bomb scare area. Billy and Fran jumped out of the car grabbing their bags and walked the last 100 yards to the George Hotel.

"See you later tonight," I said as I waved farewell.

I turned the car around and was driving down the hill when I began to think, "I wonder if Billy thought I was too scared to face the bomb?"

I immediately parked up and walked after them, catching up with them in their hotel room. We sat and chatted swapping stories, and then I left them to get some rest.

Later, around nine o'clock, I returned and sat with them in the bar. Suddenly cousins Carl and Alan appeared with arms outstretched hugging Billy and Fran warmly. So within a matter of a few hours of arriving back in England, our Yank was touching base with three of his lost family. We talked into the late hours as there was so much to catch up on.

Two days later Billy and Fran were ready for me to take

Romance without kisses

them to their next venue, which was Seckford Hall near Woodbridge. I cannot find the right words to describe my feelings to be taking my sister's son to be near where he was born, and where I had played in the grounds of the NAAFI of this grand home of Thomas Seckford, the great benefactor of Woodbridge Town. Seckford Hall proved to be magical for Billy and Fran and the task ahead for the next day was fast approaching. I had arranged for a bunch of flowers to be placed in their room; Fran extracted one bloom and arrived in the dining hall with the flower in her hand, so I had the waiter take a picture of this pre-dinner wonder.

The next day I took them both to Castle Street where Billy was born. As the Senator stood outside his birthplace, I could see the emotions spread across his face like jam on a buttered slice. I also had a job holding back my own tears because the front garden was where Billy and I had played, when he was only an English baby boy aged 3. The next adventure was to take Billy and Fran for a pint at 'The Cross', where his father Billy L and my Dad had supped many a pint in 1944. We stood with our backs against a roaring log fire, whilst the bar keeper took a picture of us. We talked Fran into trying the Suffolk Ale and after she took one sip she said, "I think I will leave the English Ale for the boys to drink."

(I can hear these words in her American accent and they make me smile even now.) Billy asked the barman if he would sell him a 'Cross' tee shirt. Billy explained to him, and he agreed how important this visit was, and he agreed to sell Billy one of the shirts, normally worn only by members of the bar staff. I explained to Billy how both our Dads had sat on this old bar bench, in side view of Pop's Café. Dad would keep one eye on his beer while watching for Mum's frantic signals that the café had suddenly become very busy. This bench is,

A Yank Returns much later On

where Lavender Rabbit had been finally dispatched. This unspoken memory ran through my mind as I drained my first pint of Adnams Ale.

After leaving the pub we all walked towards Pop's Café, which is now the 'Jade Garden', a Chinese restaurant. We stood for more pictures, which Fran obliged. Walking further up the hill we came to The Shire Hall in the square; I retold many old stories of Billy L and the family, how they had enjoyed the merriment of folks on VE day. Our tummies were now rumbling, so I asked my American kinfolk if they had ever eaten Fish and Chips.

"Well, we have never eaten English style before," Fran replied.

That was all I had wanted to hear because my thoughts had turned towards Dunwich beach, where the best fish and chips in the whole wide world are served. A fish and chip hut stands directly on the shingle beach and is where my wife, our sons and I had enjoyed many fish and chips meals.

Dunwich, Old Town is now beneath the sea; erosion had taken the town many years ago. At low tide it is said that you can still hear the church bells ring. This Suffolk coast has many magical mysteries locked away in a time warp, so I expect the winds do drift back noises from a time long ago. My memories did not need the wind to help them for I stood four square, with living recall and my lost nephew, who was now back upon the good earth of England once again. Suffolk is where my boyhood heart will remain forever and beyond.

We arrived on Dunwich beach full of expectations after our drive from Woodbridge. I had built the picture of this fish and chip venue as we drove along. I parked on the shingle beach and was somewhat surprised to find so few cars or coaches there. It had become so famous, that it was on the tourist route from as far a field as London.

Yes, even from London, coaches often dropped by for a meal, whilst travelling towards other major towns along the East Anglian coastline. I walked ahead of my visitors only to find a notice pinned on the door of the long wooden Fish and Chip hut.

Closed until the spring

We had missed the chance to eat there by one day only. With some disappointment, we strolled across the beach to the only pub open that day which is called 'The Ship'. I walked up to the bar and asked if they served fish and chips.

"Yes," came the answer.

As we waited for our meal I noticed a few familiar faces sitting and drinking. I said we had come a long way to sample the Dunwich Fish and chips.

"How far?" came a question from the drinkers.

"Oklahoma of the USA," Billy replied.

"If only we had known," said one familiar face.

It turned out that they were the actual staff from the fish and chip hut across the shingle beach.

"You missed us by just 24 hours."

As I introduced Billy and Fran to the Landlord ,up came a mighty plate of fish and chips. More ale was ordered, along with a glass of water for our Lady Fran. The meal was every bit as good as I hoped it would be. 'The Ship' did us proud that day. We returned to Seckford Hall and made arrangements to meet later in the lounge for pre-prandial drinks. We advised the restaurant that we would dine at 8pm leaving it as late as possible.

The next day we met a journalist from 'Let's Talk', an East Anglian publication. Previously, I had written a wartime story for them and got to meet the editor. All this was well before Billy had ever thought he might make the trip over. When he informed me that he and Fran

A Yank Returns much later On

would like to come to Woodbridge and see where he was born, I got in touch with the editor again, who was very interested in the Senator's story. She arranged for a journalist and a photographer to meet us at Seckford Hall to interview Billy. The journalist arrived ahead of time and we all sat in the comfortable lounge over a pot of coffee. This story made centre pages in 'Let's Talk' magazine and later in the East Anglian Times.

My hopes and prayers had been answered, completing everything I could ever have wished for. The next day I drove them all back to Gatwick where my son Peter and his family were waiting to greet them in the lounge of 'The Hilton' airport hotel. My search had now turned full circle. Luck and something wonderful had sprinkled some gold dust over a great deal of sadness in my dear sister's and Billy's lives. I feel this outcome was the best thing I had ever done for them both. Pats on the back seemed to come in several dreams after this event.

I turned to my pen again as writing had come many times to my aid during a feeling of deep loneliness. No, I was not then over my divorce. My stories were often published in 'Let's Talk' producing many ghosts from the past. People who still remembered Pop's Café wrote to me. The editor of Let's Talk asked me if there was someone I would like to get back in touch with. Only one name came to mind. It was my old sweetheart Joy Marsh. This SOS was published in the next month's magazine and was answered promptly, by one of Joy's sisters, Janet, who by some miraculous chance, was over from the States to bury her 92-year-old mother. She had wanted to take something of the past of old Woodbridge back to the States with her after the funeral. 'Let's Talk' magazine seemed a good read for her flight home. Thumbing through the pages, she came across my SOS to find a girl from my past called Joy Marsh. The chances

Romance without kisses

of her sister reading this magazine before going back home to the States seem impossible odds to calculate. She wrote to me informing me that her sister Joy had died very young and never had any children. This news came at a very low point in my life. I remember sitting in front of my computer with this letter in my hand, with tears running down my face.

"How could my lovely Joy Marsh be no more?"

Gosh, it was that kind of low moment I will never forget. If I was forced to open my store of low times, this moment would fall out. Joy Marsh was an important part of my old wartime Woodbridge story; a fine romance with no kisses. A child's first love had burnt itself deep into my very soul. Later Janet sent me a black and white picture of Joy taken at the age when we were first chums. On the picture can be seen the three sisters Janet, Joy, and Shirley along with Aunt Milly and Girly the dog and Tibbles the cat. To this day, I have it in pride of place on my office wall, near my computer where I am writing this part of my story. More gold dust had been sprinkled over me when that picture arrived, proving to me just how important it is to write down these fond private memories. Had I not written the article for 'Let's Talk', this could never have happened.

Correction.
Joy Marsh died at the age of 47 years, married with three children.

Chapter 9

Saxmundham

My first wife, Jean Window, had been evacuated to Benhall Green in 1941, around the same time of Pop's Café opened in nearby Woodbridge. Jean shared my love for Suffolk. Whenever I travel in the direction of Saxmundham I always stop and walk around the graves in St Mary's Church, Benhall, taking flowers to a couple who took Jean in as their little London Evacuee and sort of adopted her for the rest of their lives. Their names were Mr and Mrs Read. On one of my visits in 2002, I stood by their graveside for a moment looking long and hard at their headstone thinking death is so strange and in some ways it is unfair that these two wonderful Suffolk people are nothing more now than names carved on a lump of cold Portland stone. With this in mind, I decided to bring them back to life by writing a story about something of their lives and how they had opened up their home and hearts to a young girl child from London, whom I had the luck to meet and marry many years later.

Jean's story really began, one Sunday morning at St Mary's Church back in 1941. The Vicar announced from his pulpit that the Government wanted host families living in the country to take children into their homes

Romance without kisses

to help them escape the bombs of London. The Reads put their hands up and agreed to host a child and waited patiently for the evacuees to arrive. About a month after they had volunteered, the vicar called Mrs Read saying, "Ella, please come and choose a child to take home."

Ella was shocked and replied, "Vicar, I could never come and select a child like one would in a cattle market. Just bring me a little girl to my door is all I ask."

Jean had found a splendid home from home staying with a couple who ultimately loved her like their own child. Jean stayed with them for over six months and then every school holiday after, she spent her six weeks with them. When I married Jean her adopted mother and father from Benhall Green attended our wedding. I understand this was the first time that Ella or her husband had ever travelled more than 30 miles from their home in Suffolk. Herbert George Read and Ella Mary Read lived at 18 Benhall Green around three miles from the town of Saxmundham. It was a tied cottage owned by the landowner where Ella worked in service to the family. Herbie, as he was fondly called, worked on the land.

They were a childless couple but they had a favourite niece Sylvia Smith; their home reflected the hard times they lived through. Homemade carpets amounted to nothing more than a square of Hessian and cut up bits of coloured material from the ragbag. These bits of old clothing were pulled through a Hessian layer with a sacking needle and patted into order. These were wartime carpets that Ella made from time to time. Come each spring, she bashed the winter dust from them against the outside wall and then a flick of the broom over the brick floor, which trumpeted loudly, "Springtime has arrived!"

In those days, no services were laid on within the property. There was just one cold tap outside, near the

Saxmundham

back door. Nearby stood a large a timber feather-board clad washroom, built on sturdy brick foundations. A washing copper boiler stood in the corner of this outside building, along with the ubiquitous 'Wooden Dolly' (a device for agitating the water) standing on guard, awaiting a handful of kindling wood and a flame from a match to begin the Monday wash! Reckitt and Coleman's 'Dolly Blue bag' greeted each boiling wash, to bring out that perfect whiteness. Ella also cooked in this washroom on two paraffin-cooking stoves, which stood on the brick floor. These two very flat wick cookers produced some wonderful steamed suet puddings; Steak and Kidney being among my favourites. Much tender care was bestowed on these little paraffin stoves. The wicks had to be kept neatly trimmed and the brass polished bright like a soldier's helmet.

The toilet was down the garden, the 'Thunder Box' as Herbie used to call it. The wooden toilet seat was scrubbed white and the contents in the bucket were emptied daily into a large previously dug hole in the long back garden. This area of the garden was rotated each year, with vegetables growing over last year's disposals. Crop rotation, of sorts! Around the 'Thunder Box' grew tall, sweet smelling Balsam flowers. The bees loved these tall plants; you could hear them buzzing when you took your seat in the outside loo. In those days, the toilet roll, it seemed, had never been invented. It was just bits of old newspaper cut into neat 9"x5" portions and held together with rough string and hung over a nail driven into the back of the door. Recent news updates were often read in strips of 9x5 newsprint, whilst listening to the buzzing bees over the flowers growing close to the wooden hut. The 'Thunder Box' actually meets all of today's environmental considerations. Recycling our waste, maintaining a clean environment, planting flowers to encourage bees to pollinate our vegetables and fruit. Such was the outside loo at 18 Benhall Green in 1940 – 1960.

Herbie kept a few laying hens in the back garden which were Rhode Island Red x Light Sussex. This cross was known as a dual-purpose fowl. They were good layers and a table bird when their laying days were over. Old, fat hens were sought after for the wartime stew pot. In the days when I got to know Mr Read, he had some problems with bending low. So when he needed to crouch down to retrieve an egg from the inside nest box, he improvised by tying a tablespoon on the end of a broom handle. With this to hand, he would deftly pick up the newly laid egg in the spoon turning towards me with a smile on his face.

"Not a bad size Terry?"

My reply was always encouraging, although never heard. Herbie was as deaf as a post; this I was told, was due a kick to his head from a farm horse, many a year back. If you wanted to have a conversation with him, you needed pencil and paper. In the house Ella always kept small bits of plain paper to write upon, ready for such occasions. These were tucked away behind the biscuit tin ready to hand. After Ella retired from the big house where she had worked many years in service, she was offered the cottage for a very reasonable sum. She purchased it outright from her life's savings; some of it was in gold. There were sovereigns saved during years of prudence and yes, she kept them in that biscuit tin, near where the scraps of writing paper were kept.

Ella was; a joy to listen to full of country stories ,many of which I have never forgotten. One evening, Herbie came home from a day's work hoeing weeds from around crops growing in the field, with his old friend and neighbour Mr Sharman. On arriving home he grabbed a piece of paper and began writing frantically, "Why has Mr Sharman not spoken to me all day in the field?"

Ella read this note quickly and rushed to the back gate and called Mr Sharman back asking, "Herbie is very upset because he wondered if you were angry with him, as you have not spoken to him all day long?"

Mr Sharman came back towards her with a look of guilt written all over his face, "No, I have never been angry with Herbie."

The reason, he went on to explain, "I had forgotten to sand down yesterday's conversation with Herbie from my hoe handle last night."

When this was all revealed to Herbie, all three had a group hug and a hearty chuckle.

The Co-op grocer called once a week on his horse and cart. He carried a large wicker basket in which last week's order of Mrs Read's was carried. He lifted the Suffolk latch on the back door, greeting Ella warmly.

"Mrs Read, I have some special offers this week to tempt you."

This sort of conversation went on each week. Ella gave the man her latest list of things she wanted him to bring the following week. Today's delivery had been costed down to the last penny. The money was always waiting on the kitchen table but the rounds man never counted it, knowing it would be the correct amount of money when dealing with the likes of Ella.

The larder was located between the kitchen and the living room. It was large in comparison with the overall square footage of the house. The floor was tiled in traditional red Suffolk Pammet sets. Large shelves hung all around the walls with thick white marble worktops keeping the fats and cooked meats cool. Up on the shelves stood Wedgwood blue and white plates standing on edge in rows against white washed walls.

Romance without kisses

It was a place of great importance to Ella so much so that in 1960 when the council offered to connect main drainage to the cottages, Ella flatly refused! When she told me about this offer (which I had thought was heaven sent) She grabbed hold of my hand and said, "Terry, do you know where they were going to put the toilet?"

She pulled me towards her larder saying, "In there they were going to put that dirty thing!"

Herbie died aged 76. Mrs Read said,"I knew he was dying because he woke me up in the middle of the night saying, Ella I do not feel well."

She told me all this a week after his death. "You see Herbie always slept until the dawn chorus so the fact that he awoke in the middle of the night I felt his time had come."

She also found a packet of runner bean seeds on his bedside cabinet that he had intended to sow the next day. I felt very sad that this quiet man was no more, yet he had left this world full of plans for tommrow. In my old age, I am trying to adopt the same philosophy. (i.e. regardless of age, I must continue to live looking forward to a tomorrow!)

Mrs Read lived to 87; her health had begun to fade so her niece Sylvia moved her bed downstairs. Ella's favourite radio programme was *The Archers*; she only put on her large old wireless set to listen to this programme. Sylvia asked her Aunt if she would like a television; Ella was half hearted about the idea but eventually agreed as much to please her niece as herself. The television only lasted a week in the house. She asked Sylva to take it back to the shop because it invaded her other pleasures too much, like not being able to hear the hedgehog pushing the saucer of milk about the yard to get the last drop of milk, she put out every evening for it to drink. Mrs Read knew about retaining the important things in

Saxmundham

life, and had true qualities of a countrywoman.

Jean and I managed to get to Ella's funeral. Jean was in a wheelchair because her bone cancer had taken over her spine, but she insisted on walking the last few yards into the church. The funeral service was well attended by so many young children of the village, along with many neighbours and friends. The youngsters got to know Ella Read because she encouraged the children to come up her back garden to play games like Snakes and Ladders and Dominos. These board games were always available, as was Ella to play a round or two with the children, who lifted the ever unlocked back door latch.

A year later I met Sylvia in the charity shop in Saxmundham where she worked as a volunteer. I took many of Jean's bits of clothing there, after she died a year after the funeral of Mrs Read.

In her will Ella left her niece the cottage and Jean a hundred pounds along with a silver pot she had always admired when she was a young evacuee. Sylvia had the cottage gutted to modernise it, knocking down Ella's much-loved washhouse, which took so much light from the kitchen. Sylvia said, "Terry, do you think my Aunt will ever forgive me?"

I assured her Aunt Ella's museum home was far better now. Sylvia did not live very long to enjoy her refurbished home. She is also buried near Mr and Mrs Read's grave. So ending (I thought), everything connecting me with Benhall Green. I felt very lonely walking with so many ghostly memories of my childhood in Suffolk and my extended friendships touching my dear wife's life. Winston Churchill had a saying about his low moments when the Second World War was not going well, K.B.O.

"Keep Buggering On!"

In 2002 I drafted out a few pages covering Mr and

Romance without kisses

Mrs Read's life. Shortly after I sent the story to the editor of St Mary's Church Parish Magazine. I never had any response, so I assumed, incorrectly, that it had not been considered for publication. I was living at the time in Wakes Colne Essex in a small railway cottage close to the Steam Museum at the side of the line that runs between Marks Tey and Sudbury. I had forgotten all about my attempts to have the Reads returned to life from their Portland stone headstone when, as I was preparing to go out, my phone rang and a voice asked me if I was the Terry Basson who wrote about Mr and Mrs Read of Benhall Green. I replied that I was and wondered what I could do for her. She told me that she was the daughter of the new neighbours who had moved next to Mrs Read, who was by then a widow. Actually I did recall Mrs Read telling me she had new neighbours as she said they were very posh. The voice went on to explain that her Dad was a bank manager and after retirement he and Mum purchased a home in Benhall Green. She said that during visits she got to know Ella and Sylvia very well; in fact when Sylvia was refurbishing Mrs Read's cottage, she tore out the old wooden fireplace surround from the living room and threw it on the skip. The caller asked for it to be installed in her little clap-boarded house.

"What, Terry, you don't know is, I live not two hundred yards from your home!" she exclaimed.

So she invited me to come the following day for coffee at around 10am when I could see the old fireplace again that had been recovered from the skip. I jumped at the invitation; I was really excited, because I never thought I would ever touch this period again. That evening, after the phone call, I decided to polish up the Mapping and Webb silver plant holder that Ella had left in her will for her little evacuee and I wrapped it in some nice soft tissue.

Arriving at the house on time, I was greeted by a very nice lady in her late forties who invited me into her living room. There stood that pine fire surround that my whole family had sat before many a night, with a nice warm fire in the grate. She then pointed to the copper fingerplates on the doors as they were also from Mrs Read's home. I then handed her my gift.

"Gosh," she said, "how have I deserved this?"

With care, I took it from her hand and placed in on the mantel of the timber fire surround. There and then, the fireplace was now complete. This silver pot was exactly where Mrs Read had kept it all those years ago!

THE THUNDERBOX LOO!

Chapter 10

First steps into the world of work

I left school at the age of 15; a careers adviser interviewed me before my education days were over. I announced my interest in working with chickens on a poultry farm. So I was sent to Bow in Mile End, to a chicken processing plant. Plucking dead chickens was not what I'd meant when I had said, "I would like to work with chickens!"

Money was short at home and Mum wanted me out to work to help her with my upkeep. I was interviewed for a job in a tent factory. I was accepted, and my wages were 15 shillings a week. I used my bike to travel to work; Mum found me an old army shirt with two patch pockets either side and long trousers that she had shortened to fit. I still recall my first day. The foreman showed me the tent repair section, where I was put to work helping to patch old army bell tents. My job was to throw a noose over the top of the bell then winch it up high, tying it off suspended. I then looked for the entrance; in I went to open it up against the roof lights to see if I could find any holes. When I found a chink of light, I pushed a rod through the hole and a guy outside made a ring chalk

Romance without kisses

mark in order to locate the holes later. It was essential that nothing in the way of holes was ever missed. Machinists then repaired the tents in another part of the factory. It was a very dirty job and very stuffy inside these old tents. I often thought, "Goodness knows where these tents have been. On some campaign perhaps out East?"

After the first day I felt exhausted; I pedalled off home, sat in the chair and fell fast asleep. I was finally awoken by my mother's voice saying, "Terry your dinner is on the table."

This is how I spent each night for the next three weeks. From my wages, I gave ten shillings to Mother and kept five shillings in one of my shirt pockets in my army shirt. Three weeks had past when I found that I now had fifteen shillings! I'd never had so much money in my life. These savings came from not going out because I slept the sleep of the dead and could not get up any strength to spend one penny of my hard worked earnings. With my fifteen shillings, I planned to buy my mother a canary bird in a cage. I recovered from my tiredness after about three weeks and found my feet again in a world of personal choices. So with greater sophistication I chose to spend my pennies on chips and the cinema. Oh no, sadly Mum never did get her canary from me.

We were all living in Forest Gate at this time; Dad and Mum were now retired. Pop's Café number two was gone, so income from the business had ceased and Dad and Mum only had their pensions to live from. So my ten shillings a week came just in time to help support, well, at least me. Gone were the prosperous Woodbridge days and Dad often spoke about how he regretted wasting his savings on two years without work, after the original Pop's Café was sold. I also found work after the tent factory in two shops in Woodgrange Road with one being an ironmonger called 'Weedens' which

First steps into the world of work

was very like the two Ronnies shop where they sold Fork Handles! The other was called 'The Smallholders Stores'. A guy named Jack Frost owned this! Still I had no plans to train towards gaining something more useful and better paid. My last job before I was called up for my National Service was Trebor's Sweet factory. "I hit the heady heights of Van Boy!"

It was the custom that each driver had a boy allocated to him who remained his boy throughout. I still remember his name. It may be prudent if I do not include it in this book other than to say his first name was Bill.

Bill worked mostly for himself using his driver's job as a means to fulfil his other interests; stealing crates of sweets had become his dedicated pastime.

The driver and his boy were issued with a strong leather apron. Bill began my education on the very first day, "Now Terry, you must always walk about the loading bay with your hands resting in your apron, just above your waist," he explained, "You see, when the checker guy is not looking, walk towards a stack of Trebor Mints and as quick as a flash lift your apron and grab a packet, holding the sweets under the apron. That's nothing unusual, because you and I always hold our hands in this fashion, got It?"

"Yes Bill like this?" I replied.

This is how I became inducted into Bill's world of crime. Actually I never thought of it as a crime, more as a challenge to be like driver Bill, who had greatly impressed me for some strange unexplainable reason.

These stolen packets of sweets were picked up on random walks around the stockpiles of sweets, close to the loading bays. After about a week stealing in this casual way Bill then took me further into his confidence.

It turned out that the Checker was also on the fiddle with Bill and other drivers I guess. The real sting was to steal crates of sweets, containing six jars. We waited for the times when the checker went to the loo or was called away on the phone by another department. Bill and I swiftly moved from the back of the van. With me wheeling the sack truck, as quickly as a wink, six crates were placed into the van before the checker returned. Bill's stolen sweet store was kept in the front section of the van that was kept empty for returning crates. A partition within the back of the van kept the swag from the sight of the checker. On one occasion this area was stacked with stolen sweets. We were about to shut up the back of the van that was full up to the tailboard, when suddenly the checker came out waving an invoice saying, "You must get another few crates on because it was a last minute urgent order."

"Sorry mate we are full!" Bill shouted.

The checker looked a little confused. He jumped off the loading bay and pulled up the shutter to the empty crate compartment.

As he pulling up the roller door he said, "Put the urgent order in here."

Then in a shocked breath because of what he had discovered he said, "You crafty Bastards!"

He could not report us because he also had a crate or two on board with the main load for a split. The outcome was simple; the checker wanted cutting in on the front load as well. Bill was very angry indeed!

Bill taught me a lot about holding my nerve. One day the checker disappeared from the loading area. Bill did the usual thing. Quickly he wheeled the sack truck to a stack of crates. I banged down two on the barrow, when suddenly the manager's head appeared, he looked towards us, I whispered to Bill,

"Our game is up."

Bill said, as cool as a cucumber,

First steps into the world of work

"Put another two crates on top of the first two Terry."

We then strolled back with four stolen crates to the van. The manager took in this scene as being perfectly normal, because we had not looked flustered or in too much of a hurry, thanks to Bill's steady intervention. Whenever I watch the film Oliver, with Bill Sykes teaching him how to pick a pocket or two, I see how vulnerable Oliver was and I think of myself with my Bill. Actually, like Oliver, I hardly profited from this illegal activity, other than a few bob (shillings) Bill gave me from time to time.

Trebors sent sweets all over England so often we would be away for one or two nights. Before we left the depot, the driver went to the office to draw what was called, 'Night Out Money'. The driver was given enough money to get a bed and breakfast for himself and enough for buying grub for both of us. The van boy was expected to sleep in the cab. We often went towards the West Country stopping overnight in Honiton. Drivers knew the best places to stay. Tiny's place was one of them. Tiny was, of course, a huge man weighing in over 25 stone. His wife Joan was really the tiny one. It was a large farmhouse with a great big kitchen and open log fire. The food was hot and plentiful. We shared our evening meal with other truck drivers, sitting around a big table telling stories. The conversations mostly spoke about how many drops their companies expected them to do, within the time they were allowed, in order to be back ready to load up once more.

With the van boys' tummies now full, off we toddled back to the lorry park. Tiny's parking place was up the hill in a field, which was fine in the summer, but in the winter it was another story. The hot food in our stomachs lasted about a hundred yards then we felt frozen, so with cold hands we went to our respective lorries. With their windows iced up we huddled down under blankets trying to get to sleep.

My mother used to say, "Terry you can fall asleep on a clothes line!" But the freezing conditions in the field park were too difficult to allow me to drift into my dreams. When conditions were so severe, tiny Joan would make the long track to the lorries with just an oil lamp in her hand. Banging on the side of the frozen cabs, sometimes past-midnight, she would say, "Come on boys, I cannot let you sleep out on a night such as this."

A dozen freezing boys quickly gathered themselves up; our Florence Nightingale led us back to the farm. Regardless of the late hour, Joan served us hot soup from her stockpot, which she kept warm the whole day and night. We each found a soft chair before a crackling log fire and soon fell asleep, dreaming of our lady with the lamp.

I rarely ate sweets whilst working at Trebors, being among so much sugar turned me off, so to speak. My van boy days lasted up to the age of 18 until the day came to sign up for my National Service.

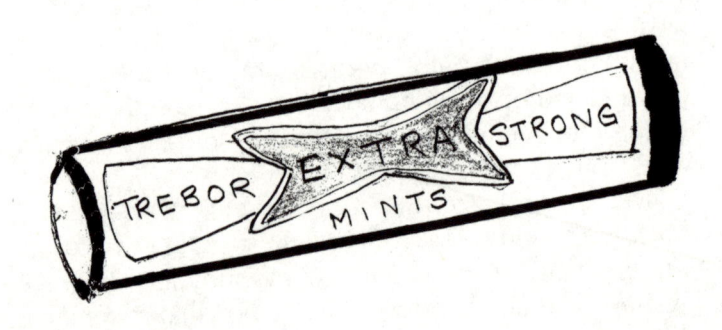

Chapter 11

National Service

At the turn of my 18th birthday, I was required to sign up to do my National Service, initially for a period of 18 months. About two months later the government extended it by another six months, making a total of two years, which felt like an eternity out of my young life! I felt it was almost a prison sentence, perhaps for my misdemeanors in my Trebor days!

I did my initial six weeks training in Winchester. The army came as a shock to all of us. We joined as 'Teddy Boys' with narrow bottom trousers (known as drain pipes), long hair, and my suit had a velvet collar! I had thick crêpe-soled shoes, which we called 'brothel creepers'. After we were issued with all our kit, we were asked to parcel up our civvies and send them home. Haircuts, teeth examinations and health checks were carried out; but they never actually examined our hooves, but to our surprise this came much later. When we were on parade, the officer asked us to lift one boot, just as if we were one of Dad's horses, and the sergeant counted how many studs we had. If the boot had one missing, we were on a charge!

Romance without kisses

In the left hand pocket of our battle dress, we were obliged to carry our AB 64 part 1 book being very much like a small passport, which contained all our personal information birth date, next of kin and even a will in case we were killed in action. Woe betide those who had forgotten to put this document into their pocket. The discipline was extreme, so we became broken Teddy Boys, to such an extent that one lad did have a complete breakdown. Sometimes very hurtful things were done for no reason at all, such as when the mail call was sounded when we eagerly waited to see if we had a letter from home. The Corporal walked into our barrack room, which in my case was on the first floor, checking the mail and then shouting out a soldier's name and giving him his mail. One day it was my turn to engage his need to show power over us so, when I called, "Over here Cpl," he looked in my direction then threw my letter out of the window. I had to dash downstairs to retrieve it. We never knew who was going to receive this treatment next, but we all knew we just had to 'grin and bear it' otherwise he would have found other ways to make our lives hell.

We were all home-sick after a week and we were not allowed out of the camp until our six weeks training was over. Unknown to us at that time our tea was dosed with Bromide, which reduced our libido to zero; this Bromide was stopped after our training was complete.

Actually I was still a virgin soldier at 18 as I never thought of myself as being attractive to women, because older relatives often mentioned that I had a baby face. After our basic training was over, we were allowed out into Winchester town. I walked up into the green meadows above the town to stretch my legs and to look back at the stunning views of the town from such a vantage point. I met a girl doing the same thing, I offered her a fag, she accepted and we talked and walked further up the hill. We decided to sit and talk for a bit more. I really liked the look of her, so, I kissed her!

"Wow," I thought,

I was so bold to have taken the plunge. We stayed together and walked back to the town to have a coffee. By this time it had got dark; she walked towards the barracks with me passing the Cathedral. We stopped against the ancient walls and snogged more seriously. It was a bitter cold day so I had on my army greatcoat which was a bugger to steam press because it was so thick.

I had intercourse against those walls of the Cathedral but when I asked her how it was for her, she replied,

"What do you mean?"

"Well you know what we have just done. You know sex," I replied

She looked at me strangely, "Not with me you haven't!" she said.

This started to alarm me, until I realized that I had just had sex with my greatcoat! My thick army overcoat came in very handy when I was cold and lonely!

We received orders to be transferred to a place called Munster in Germany where I spent the rest of the two years of my life along with 600 young men. When we arrived the Technical Adjutant interviewed my group, one at a time. His name was Captain Stileman, who enquired if I was happy in this regiment.

"No Sir I am not." I replied.

He looked up from his paperwork a little surprised, clearly my answer seemed unusual to him.

"Why is that?" he said.

"Well Sir I wanted to learn to drive and not to become a foot soldier in the infantry."

"We do have drivers here you know, Rifleman Basson."

He went on to explain that he needed a replacement driver, because the driver who had been with him throughout WW2 was getting de-mobbed.

"Look Basson, I will put you on a driving course. I am the officer who passes successful drivers. If I pass you, then you can become my driver."

I learnt to drive a Halftrack and a Willy's American jeep. Captain Stileman gave me a first class pass mark after the twelve-week course and good to his word, I became his driver.

I then moved to Headquarter Company sharing a room with seven other guys. My duties were to drive the Captain and his wireless operator out on manoeuvres, which were generally held near the Black Forest. The Captain hated the Germans, treating them like second-class citizens. No doubt the war years had something to do with his attitude towards them. I recall, on one occasion we were driving along a road ahead of some heavily armoured tanks. He lent over to his wireless operator and told him to instruct the tank commander to turn off the road across a field of wheat. The tanks spun off the road and tore up the field of corn completely destroying the crop. Without concern, he ordered them across other fields of vegetables; he had complete disregard for how they were affecting the German farmers' income. On another occasion, he ordered our section to take over the out-buildings of a farmyard and bed down for the night. The farmer came out of his home shouting angrily at him. Captain Stileman walked up to him, with his face within spit of the German's face and shouted loudly, "Do you know you are talking to a British officer!"

I got to meet his old wartime driver who was being de-mobbed and asked him about his Captain. He said, "Oh him, yes Terry, on one occasion he killed a German soldier with his bare hands. Strangled him to death he did. He hates the Bastards."

How sad it is, when war changes so much in us. I looked upon the Captain with different understanding eyes after that bit of information. My Captain was promoted from Technical Adjutant to Company Commander; he was so taken up with his new position that he forgot all about his Jeep and me. So little was the vehicle used that I actually jacked it up in the motor pool, taking all four wheels off, and just kept it greased up. I had nothing to do, which pleased me. So I took up going to the NAAFI to play snooker for hours on end. It was a very different sort of play from those early days in Seckford Hall with no Dad there to guide me. One day I was walking passed the parade ground when the Captain appeared in the road. I threw him a salute as we passed each other. Then he turned back towards me and said, "Basson what are you doing with yourself these days?"

To which I replied, "Playing snooker mostly, Sir."

He stood for a moment in deep thought, then said, "Basson I think it would be helpful if you would go over to my married quarters daily to help in the house."

When my mates heard about this they said, "Jammy Sod!"

I reported next day to the Captain's home but sadly I could not use the jeep on missions like this. The distance between the camp and the officer's quarters was about two miles. I assumed the round trip of four miles would be once a day but I was required by the Captain's wife to return to the barracks for my midday meal; thus my daily duties caused me to walk eight miles per day. When I arrived at his home for the first time, Mrs Stileman opened the door to me and I told her, that the Captain has sent me. She replied by asking me my name. I told her it was Terry, but she wanted to know my surname of Basson and from that time on, that was how she addressed me.

Romance without kisses

It was my first encounter of an 'Upstairs, Downstairs' relationship with a woman. She certainly was a person enjoying her husband's position. In situations like this, an army officer's wife would assume the rank of her husband. In modern terms that was a 'learning curve' for me. It seemed that the lower ranking officers' wives were more likely to do this. Many of the other senior officers' wives, who were accustomed to rank and wealth, used my first name. They didn't need to demonstrate such power over me, as they had probably had servants and chauffeurs in their private lives, back home.

Sometimes I would have to do the journey three times as I was engaged as a waiter for dinner parties, given for other officers and their wives. I had to learn how to wait at table and to perform 'silver service'. My training took place at their home when they were eating alone. They had a dinner service with plates designed for male or female guests. On the ladies' plates were traditionally dressed Dutch women and the men's plates had Dutch men. I had to make sure that the Dutch people were standing upright when I placed the plate in front of the guests. Their housekeeper/servant/cook was called Marianna. She was German with the cost of her upkeep and salary being underpinned by the German Government, as was the cost of the very nice house where the Captain and his family lived.

Marianna was a great cook and one of her specialities was a sherry trifle to die for. This, as I recall was only prepared for the times when they had formal dinner parties. I had to go to the Officers' Mess in Headquarter Company to borrow a waiter's white coat. This was fastened, with regimental buttons from The King's Royal Rifle Corps, right up to a collar around the neck. My duties started on arrival at least half an hour before the guests were due. When the door-bell rang, it was my job to open it and greet the guests, take their coats and show them into the lounge. There were double glass, sliding doors between the dining room and the lounge. The dining room was dimmed and I lit the candles. Marianna's meal was always delivered to the dining room on a trolley pushed through the hall by me. I waited until Marianna told me the first course was ready to be served and then I walked into the dining room, opening the two glass sliding door then announced in my best formal voice, "Dinner is served."

I was taught that a waiter should be unseen by the guests. This I managed reasonably well until one time I dropped a potato from my silver service serving spoons, managing to land it in a partly drunk glass of wine! I felt the Captain's eyes staring at me and began to wonder what my penalties might be for this error. But the Captain and his wife didn't reprimand me this time.

After the guests retired back into the lounge I started to clear the table loading all of the dishes onto the trolley. I was always hoping that some of the trifle had been left in the bowl. Marianna was also hoping for the same thing, so I had an extra helping by eating as much as I could from the trolley as I wheeled it back to the kitchen. I should have felt guilty, as when I arrived there Marianna always shared what was left between us equally.

Life continued this way with my duties including lawn cutting, hedge trimming and other garden work. During the summer Marianna would call me in for some homemade lemonade. I was getting rather 'fed up' with this work, which didn't feel like being a soldier but at the same time I didn't think anyone would listen if I complained. In 1953 the Captain's wife returned to the UK for the Queen's Coronation leaving her husband in charge of the household. It was one day, during this time, when the Captain was away from home, that Marianna asked me if I would like to see her embroidery. She took me to her bedroom and showed me this delicate work she was doing, when suddenly I heard the front door open and the Captain shouted, "Marianna! Basson!"

Marianna was petrified and asked me to hide behind the door. I decided that we were doing no wrong so I opened the door and out we walked with her in front of me. The Captain was angry with us at the thought that we were having sex as he was absent, so in tones of anger he ordered me outside to stand by his car, at the same time telling Marianna to get on with her work. I waited as he had asked then the Captain came out, taking off his stiff cap he hit the bonnet of the car loudly saying, "What were you doing in that girl's room?"

I was standing to attention and in a quiet voice responding to his anger, I replied, "Looking at her embroidery, Sir."

He repeated his question several times as he was unwilling to accept my answer, but I stuck to my true story. He threatened that I would be thrown into the Guard Room but I remained standing upright as I had nothing more to say. His anger seemed to subdue, when he said that I might well have been looking at her embroidery, but when an officer comes home, he does not expect to find his driver and housekeeper together in her bedroom. He turned on his heel and drove back to camp leaving Marianna and I with red faces; this incident was almost forgotten, I thought. Mrs Stileman returned from England and no doubt the Captain told her all about the incident. A month later, on a Summer's day, I was cutting the grass when I heard Marianna call out as if in distress. I ran to the kitchen to find she had fainted and was lying on the floor. Mrs Stileman also heard the scream and she phoned for an ambulance from the Royal Military Hospital, less than a mile away. Mrs

Stileman concluded that I was guilty of making Marianna pregnant and stopped her casual conversations with me. The Captain, shortly after, called me to his office and said, in no uncertain terms that I was to stop fraternizing with his maid. Marianna was not pregnant but found to be diabetic and had collapsed in a coma. There was never an apology for not believing that,

"I WAS LOOKING AT HER EMBROIDERY!"

This situation hit me hard. I could no longer talk to the maid and the Captain and his wife were very cool towards me. I talked this situation over with a Colour Sergeant who was in charge of the stores and the Armory in the Headquarter block. He was shocked to hear that the Captain was using me for domestic duties and said that I did have a good basis for complaining about him. This strengthened my resolve to a point that I should speak to Captain Stileman, but I was still very subservient and continued to oblige and continue with my work. My opportunity arose when, on another summer's day, the Captain drove up to his home and asked me, "How are you getting on these days, Basson?"

I had just finished mowing the lawn with a push mower that was blunt and difficult to move, so with sweat on my brow mingled with determination I replied, "Well Sir, I am not happy with this work."

In amazement and sarcastically he replied, "Oh, so you are not happy, with us. OK, I will send you back to a Duty company."

This threat was to try to make me change my mind, but his was the mood that changed when I continued to tell him that I had shared my concerns, about my workload, to Colour Sergeant Shreeve. It dawned on him that his game was up, as during the months I had been working for him I had not been employed properly and

Romance without kisses

he could be in trouble, himself, if it all came out. Colour Sergeant Shreeve had said that the Captain had no right to treat me as an extra servant, when I was a soldier and so had there been an investigation, he would have been in trouble. This saga was now over.

I obtained a position in the Headquarter Company Stores, not in an active duty company the Captain had threatened, gained a stripe and had full responsibility for the Armory. I enjoyed working with Colour Sergeant Shreeve and on many Sundays would accompany him on a 'rough shoot', shooting wild game as we walked. His wife packed us sandwiches but as an inexperienced young soldier I forgot my place by thinking we were mates. Suddenly his casual mood changed; he made me stand to attention as he quickly reminded me, that he was a non-commissioned officer and that I must remember my junior rank. Nevertheless, he remained a kind and supportive Sergeant to me. I became quite proficient in rifle shooting and obtained the badge of marksman, which was sewn on to my sleeve; I became part of the Battalion Rifle Team. It was good for me, and good for him, to have a member of his staff, who was a keeper of the arms and a good shot too. Of course he was unaware that from the age of nine I had my own air rifle, so I quickly became an efficient member of this rifle team. Later, I was part of the successful team representing our Battalion at a B.A.O.R.(British Army Over the Rhine) competition and we won silver spoons as our prize for the best army shooting team over the Rhine. The spoons with Lions on the handles, were sent to me after de-mob and I believe my son, David, still has them.

Many years later, at the age of 75, my love of shooting was rekindled when I visited a Country Game Fair in Wiltshire. There was a Clay Pigeon shoot and I stepped up to try my luck. With applause from all around I was delighted to have hit every clay pigeon and was so proud of myself.

On the back of the door of our steel lockers in Germany, we kept a de-mob calendar for our last year. The 365 boxes resembled a spider's web starting from the outside and moving towards the middle to the magic day. Daily we shaded in each square and, rather like the rabbits in the cornfields during harvest all those years ago, we isolated the remaining days in the centre.

My draft collected together beside a three ton truck, after breakfast on our last day. It was always there on a Saturday as this truck was the de-mob one, which we had watched enviously for nearly two years. Our last day in Germany came; saying goodbye to our friends was a tearful event as they still had time to do. We returned to Winchester and for some reason had to stay there for a further two weeks until our documentation had been finalized. Our draft 2267 departed from Winchester to Liverpool Street; as we left the train, we were saying goodbye to each other along the platform; at the ticket barrier, a sergeant was standing. When we reached him, he asked if we were draft 2267 and we replied that we were. We were shocked to be told that we had to travel, on another truck, to Davis Street London, which is where the Regimental Offices were and still are located. We thought the army was all over for us but our group stood in a room smoking, when a sergeant walked in and said, "Fags out! Officer on parade!"

We were then informed that we had a further two years on reserve service before us. An empty kit bag was thrown at us and we had to go through the procedure of drawing all our kit again. I, eventually, arrived home with a kit bag on my shoulder, to be greeted by my family. It had been a long two years away from home, and in some ways I regret this period. I was left with the

Romance without kisses

impression that all officers had educated voices ,so in turn all educated voices came from people in authority and they would be the ones to order me around, in the civilian world just as they did during those two years. I bore this stupid idea for at least ten years after de-mob.

It might have been thought that nearly two years in Germany would have, at least, have made me learn something of their language and culture. But in the true British style and because we were 600 British all together, I left with only three sentences to start my German Phrase book of the future. I will share them with you as they may come in handy one day. They are probably not grammatically correct but they gave me the right results.

Well, for the first two they did, the last one I must keep as my secret!

1. I was hungry and always wanted second helpings in the cookhouse but when I asked for more (in English) the German ladies refused. Then I spotted another soldier getting more because he had asked in German. So I quickly learned that, like Oliver, if you are still hungry and you want to ask for more please you could say,
"Hast Du noch mehr bitte?"

2. We obtained cigarettes very cheaply and so to make some money we sold them on to Germans when their supply was short. During our 12-week driving course, travelling beyond the camp, gave us the opportunity to sell thousands. I can never forgive the British cigarette companies for turning so many of us into addicts, under the fraudulent mask of being kind to the troops, when they sold them so cheaply. With my son Peter's death being linked to smoking it still haunts me today. But, the sentence I used then was,

"I have a hundred cigarettes for sale. One mark twenty for 20."
"Ich habe ein hundert Zigaretten zu verkaufen. Eine Mark zwanzig für zwanzig."

3. The last was an attempt at finding accommodation for the night ! Simply it asked,
   "You and I sleep? Yes?"
   I will have to leave you wondering what the answer was (or answers were)!
   "Du und ich schlafen? Ja?"

My country had taken two years of my life, returning me aged 20 to Civvy Street, with no more than the rank of van boy for Trebor Sweets. But, if I had returned to that job, I could have been the driver now I had a licence. Would I have turned that profession into an honest one?

We will never know, but I like to think I would have changed from Bill's style of working!

Modern technology took over much later in the 21st Century, when I was delighted 'to be found' by some fellow soldiers from my draft, on the 'Forces Re-united' website and I cherish the fact that I am able to communicate with John Nash and Ken Mann. Somehow it seems so much more rosy now!

Chapter 12

Climbing the ladder

When thinking about what I should call this chapter I came up with this title. So, I will tell how I tentatively took my first chance steps towards improving my skill base.

It came about as most things had in my life, without any planning. My young wife's father was a ship's plumber who worked for The Royal Mail lines; Fred was a quiet man with a dry wit and we got on together and almost from the start we became good friends. I married his daughter at the age of 21, Jean was just 18.

I was always useful with my hands and he recognised this. My plumbing career really started with Fred, who took me under his wing and taught me his trade. This chance meeting was to give me the start, which seemingly had escaped me since leaving school. My apprenticeship lasted over three years, before I felt sufficiently confident to begin a little building business, fitting sink units and new bathrooms. I then went to night school and became trained as a heating engineer. I became an approved fitter for the National Coal Board, during the time when all houses had to have overnight burners capable of burning smokeless fuels. This work proved essential and gave me a workflow and regular work during a time when the children were growing up.

From this beginning I built a sound little business, which took me to meet other tradesmen. I met a bricklayer and a carpenter who both brought me into their contracts to carry out the plumbing side of the work. Another source of work came from a builders' merchant with a showroom in the Walthamstow High Street. They handed out my business cards to customers who wanted a plumber to fit their central heating or new bathroom suites. Sometimes my single pair of hands had difficulty satisfying my job calendar. This balance is a freelancer's nightmare. Working all day, following up leads in the evening, estimating and producing quotations was a fulltime job. My wife Jean was the base that kept our lives orderly. She helped me with the paperwork and took calls from customers, alongside taking and collecting the kids from school. So come the weekend we were very tired but solvent. This was the pattern of my working life and would have remained so, until a friend told me about opportunities to work for Housing Associations who, with the aid of government grants, were refurbishing homes to rent to those on council waiting lists for accommodation.

I took a bold step and went for an interview presenting my company with a staff of one to them. I did not tell them that I was a one-man band, so they forwarded my application to a group of surveyors who managed their work for them, preparing drawings and supervising works on site. I spoke to my friendly bricklayer and the carpenter who employed my skills from time to time saying, "If I do manage to get this big work would you consider forming a building company with me?"

To my joy they agreed. Later that month I was sent plans to refurbish a small house in West Ham. With the

Climbing the ladder

prospect of larger work I formed a company calling it T. Basson and Sons Co Ltd. My new partners accepted my name because I was the person who had contacted this source of work and had placed my business card for consideration towards the Housing Association. T. Basson and Sons, now had a staffing level of three. I chose these mixed trades as being the basic skills I needed to refurbish old properties.

We won our first job having gone into competition with two other building firms on the Association's approved list of contractors. I collected the keys to this empty house, started stripping out the property single handed with a skip in the street to take the rubbish. My two partners still had small jobs to finish before they could join me in this new enterprise. The surveyor's group informed me that they would be sending one of their staff to the property to see the progress we were making with our first job. I recognised that my single set of hands working to strip out the property would not make a good impression. This was in my mind when I opened up the house on the allotted day the surveyor's visit was to happen. Next door to the empty house sat a retired old man sitting on the window sill, reading his newspaper. I asked him if he wanted to earn a day's pay.

"What?" he asked.

I repeated the offer again.

"Son, I haven't done a days work for ten years, he replied."

To this I said, "Pop, all I want you to do is to go upstairs and make a noise with a hammer, when I tip you the wink. You can sit upstairs in this house reading that paper until you hear me cough loudly. Then start hammering on the floor."

He took up my offer; the surveyor arrived about half an hour later. Actually, all he wanted to see was that the work had been started. I shook his hand and coughed loudly. Sure enough my retired OAP started to use his hammer to great effect. I paid the old man off after the agent left then went up to the local greasy spoon to have a well earned, hot cup of tea and bacon Sarnie!

Our first job went very well and we finished the refurbishment in three months. The only problem was cash flow, as gone were the days when at the end of a week your customer paid up. With large jobs such as we had with the Housing Association, we needed to work a month before their surveyor issued us with a certificate for completed work; this took another two weeks before cheques dropped onto the mat. We all went without wages and begged and borrowed from our relations to tide us over.

I started the business without any capital; we opened credit accounts with several building suppliers. We were completely financially exposed, so we put our heads down and worked very long hours. With the major work complete, all three wives came and cleaned up the place, getting it ready for handover to the supervising surveyor, in the company of someone from the Housing Association. Our hopes were high because we had produced a wonderful refurbishment to be proud of, as thankfully so were our employers!

We traded for another six years and at one time employed ten other tradesmen and labourers. We had built up a good name with the housing trust who often used us to set examples to other builders working for them. We were the show house which stood for good work completed on time. Our largest contract was in Hackney. We produced sixteen self-contained flats from two houses adjoining each other. I found out much later from the chief executive, who liked to come around during our time on site, that the council thought it impossible to refurbish this project within a budget sum of money. This made sense, so had passed up the opportunity, waited for an unwary Housing Authority to take on the task and watch them fail.

The chief executive of the 'London Housing Assocation' decided to approach my company, with nothing more than a set of plans, and asked us to give him a price to produce sixteen units of accommodation. This was a cost cutting exercise, saving a professional writing up a very involved specification of work. So with nothing other than the plans before us we produced an estimate that was finally accepted. This was a great leap of faith by us and the HA. They were also in danger of being exposed, because they may not have asked for enough money, from The Housing Corporation, to complete this project.

Our risk was based on my very professional workforce, who knew something about refurbishing property and us getting our costing right. Having said all this, we took a great chance as this proved to be a nine-month contract in which many things could have gone wrong. The Housing Director came on site a little more regularly during the nine months; he was a surveyor before he became Chief Executive. He was always in the company of a young Housing Officer named John Clark.

We were nearing the end of the work, naturally keeping a watchful eye that the contract sum would cover all of our bills, which was tricky because without a specification no variations could be claimed for. My calculations suggested that our profits were going to be very slim. With this in mind I was in a very thoughtful worried mood when the Director walked on site.

"Mr Basson you look worried!"

I blurted out my concerns to him. He then asked what extra sum would make me happy, to which I replied,

"A thousand pounds sir."

He did not hesitate, "Granted!"

This extra thousand pounds paid our bills but left very little in the way of profit; to be frank I think we were better tradesmen than businessmen. The Mayor of Hackney was invited to the grand opening of these sixteen flats and we made the local papers, that praised our splendid work.

With a great reputation that never actually produced more than a wage for the directors, who after all were just working principals, arguments became common between us. With me in deep thinking mode about the future of the company, there came an opportunity from a chance conversation with Mr John Clark who said, "Terry there is a job in our surveying department on offer, give it some thought."

At our next board meeting of T. Basson and Sons, I discussed the possibility of my leaving the company to work for a Housing Association. My partners agreed for me to depart, saying they would continue trading with the same name. I guess sharing future profits by two, instead of three, featured a lot in their agreement to let me go.

I applied for the job in the surveyor's department and got the job of surveying building defects, in their existing tenanted housing stock. On my first day I felt like a fish out of water as working alongside office boys had never been my scene. After three days of tension thinking that everybody was so much more acquainted with their work than me, I collapsed at home. My wife called the doctor who diagnosed high blood pressure. This was directly related to my new job and my not knowing how I could conquer my feelings of inadequacy. I returned to work on the next Monday with the excuse of having a cold. The Chief surveyor instructed me to take a look at a four-storey property that had suffered from continual leaks from hot water cylinders, particularly in the ground floor units.

I felt a little more relaxed out of the office, but when I returned the Chief Surveyor asked me why I had taken so long out of the office. I looked at him somewhat in surprise. I went on to explain that I had inspected the problem and found that the cold-water tank was located high up on the roof of this tall property. The reason for continual leaks from the lower hot water cylinders was because they were not of a sufficiently strong gauge to take this pressure from the cold-water tanks on the roof.

He seemed impressed with my diagnosis then added, "Why did it take you so long?"

I told him that I had drained down the defective hot water cylinder, made a temporary repair by soldering up the split seams and restored the hot water until a new upgraded cylinder was ordered. He looked stunned and said, "Terry, you are here to diagnose building defects and instruct others to do the work. Not to do the work yourself!"

The next day I took my bag of tools out of my car and became what was expected of me, yet my troubles continued. I was sent to inspect a basement flat that had rising damp problems. I knew the problem and solution as I had cured many of these during my refurbishment days. Yet, when I picked up the pen to specify the cure my hand froze with fear. The assistant chief surveyor, back in the office, noticed this. He was a kindly man and realised how unaccustomed I was to office work. He went on to advise me just to write down what I would expect to read from a surveyor's specification to deal with the problem. You see, I could do everything necessary myself, including the waterproof re-plastering, nothing fazed me on the trade aspects. Writing all this down as an instruction was another matter. With kindness the assistant chief surveyor gently coached me, and my work began to shine.

Now I felt I was producing a worthwhile day's work which had taken me many months to come to terms with. I started to look about me at the other surveyors in the office whom I had looked up to during those awful early days. I realized that I was head and shoulders above them, because I had my trade experience behind me while none of them had such a background.

I had joined the Association at a time of restructuring and was sent as the technical advisor, to work in a housing office in the Portobello Road area. My boss was now the housing manager. The old centralised Surveying Department had a poor name among the housing staff as repairs took ages and the Chief Surveyor often came up with his familiar saying, "The only good tenant is a dead tenant!"

He was a funny old chap, yet this attitude towards tenants' repair complaints eventually underpinned a changed structure. When he was informed that building defects were going to be handled locally he announced, "Their yearly budgets will be spent in a month!"

The chief surveyor's fears never arrived. After three months working in the surveyor's office I had learnt three things. The first was to write a specification and tender the work according to the regulations of the Association. My second learning curve was how to observe irregularities. My third was really a determination that if ever I got control of the budget and the staff in this department, I could see how I would implement many changes. My move to an area Housing Management office gave me everything I had hoped for. My first day proved very exciting. On the reception counter a notice to the tenants was posted, saying any questions about late repairs could now be directed towards the Maintenance Manager, now housed in an office along the passage. I stood in this office with just a pen and bits of paper; at this point I did not have any staff. The management doors were opened for tenants to come in and pay their rents. Suddenly a guy opened my office door and asked me, in very angry terms, when his mother's fallen ceiling was going to be fixed. I smiled and tried to explain that this was my first day. Repair records had not yet arrived over from the centralised Surveyor's office. I think I was dropped into this black hole to fail. The tenant's son grabbed me by the throat and banged me against the office wall.

"Look Mate, I do not want to hear about your problems because I have plenty myself. I took my mother in because of the state of her flat. For six weeks I have put up with her and she is driving me MAD!"

He released his tight grip on me after he had blurted out his troubles; I promised him that I would give high priority to the work of replacing his mother's ceiling. The tenants now had a face at which to grumble; it was my face that they spat their frustration at. The old Surveyor had a rule never to talk to a tenant so the Housing Officers were now glad to have me with them. They had put up with this sort of abuse because few, in the surveyor's office, cared a hoot about the time it took to complete reported tenant repairs.

It took me three months to recruit some good staff starting with a secretary and then I directly employed a plumber to deal with any urgent leaks. I sacked all the contractors who had been working too closely with the old surveyor's staff. I now engaged a dozen contractors who were approved by me. I introduced value for money, plus the repairs were done within time. A new world order happened around the Paddington area office; our property existed within an easy walk from the area office.

Romance without kisses

The Association had around 900 units of accommodation housed within delightful Victorian property, which after refurbishment made wonderful flats.

Our tenants were all taken straight from the local borough's housing list; we never selected anyone. Yes, we had a mixed bunch of people, but our accommodation fell along streets of other homeowners. This made our tenants feel like individuals, unlike a council housing estate. Finding and dealing with building defects was my game, but eventually I learnt about our tenants and I got to know much about their struggles, as well about their building defects.

Tenants can be noisy complainers. I heard a row going on in the reception where the rents are collected. Suddenly my office door burst open and a Housing Officer came in saying, "Terry, please come to reception; a tenant refuses to leave until she has spoken with you.

Thinking this must be a very important problem, I spoke to her as she was very upset and told me that she has lots of flies in her bathroom. Our Victorian flats often had interior windowless bathrooms so her complaint was rather strange. I began to think that she was possibly a crank or disturbed mentally. I assured her that I would get someone to look at the problem within the hour. I phoned one of our contractors and asked him to send a guy immediately. Unfortunately, he said that all his workman were out of the office and all he had beside him was his seventeen year old son, who was useless with tools.

"No probs," I said. "Send him with a few tools which he will not need to use; all he has to do is look at some flies in the bathroom."

The contractor thought this was a strange request but with a smile, he sent his young son around, just to appease the lady. About an hour passed when my office door burst open again, there stood the seventeen year old with a red face.

"Come and see Mr Basson."

Putting down some important work I followed him to the tenant's bathroom. Indeed there was an unusual load of flies.

The tenant jumped at me, and said, "Mr Basson, you must move me from this flat." At the same time she pointed to a huge snake in her bath. It was a Boa Constrictor, but fortunately it was dead!

The lad went on to say that when he arrived he could see flies coming from the internal fan on the ceiling. To placate the tenant he agreed to take the fan down but as he removed the last screw out dropped this huge snake right into the bath. He and the tenant both screamed and he ran to me. Come see indeed! It was the last thing anyone could have imagined. Our tenant said that she could never bath in there again, adding, "Just imagine, if that snake had dropped from the ceiling whilst I was taking a bath, the fright would have killed me."

The two of us, on hearing this message, could only agree with her; this became the talk of the office and other tenants got to hear about it whilst standing at the rent desk. One conversation went a bit like this.

"Oh! That's where it went," said one lady.

"What went where?" said the housing officer behind the counter.

"My Snake," she replied.

"Your Snake?"

"Yes he is really my pet, I live on the top floor flat and I have developed a habit, on a sunny morning, of pushing open the roof access hatch and lifting him onto the apex roof, to warm up in the sun. Normally he just laid and enjoyed himself, then to my surprise he went missing."

In fact, what had happened was that the snake went walkabout and found one of the many four-inch ventilation pipes, which stuck out of this inverted roof from the lower flats. He must have dropped down one until his head came up against the fan. Unable to reverse, he died and his body began to rot. I, eventually, persuaded the terrified tenant that the tenant above would never keep another snake. It would surprise anyone to learn that flat dwellers do keep the most odd pets. Large tropical spiders were amongst them.

I spent six years in this area office. Our tenants waved at staff as they went walk-about getting on with their lives. Yes, our tenants understood that we were there to help them in so many ways. I was privileged to work with so many talented staff that eventually went onto senior positions throughout the Voluntary Housing Movement. I cannot fully understand why this group of people excelled in so many ways but for me, it proved so encouraging.

Our tenants came from all walks of life. We had Edith Vogel who had a basement flat in Moorhouse Road; she was a famous concert pianist and I understand she played on Radio Four. Above her lived a lovely Scottish couple whose name now sadly escapes me. I was called to examine a reported building fault to the top flat. So I rang the main entrance door leading to the common staircase and as I passed the upper ground floor unit, the Scottish lady tenant opened her door, saw me and said, "Mr Basson, have you some time to spare to talk to my husband? He is very sick and will die soon."

I walked into the lounge and found Jock was laying on a made up bed in his sitting room. Jock greeted me warmly and said, "Mr Basson did the wife tell you I am dying?"

Climbing the ladder

"Well, she said you were unwell Jock," I replied.

"Then would you share a wee dram of Whisky with mee?" he asked.

The room was all decorated ready for Christmas, with a very large red Poinsettia, which set this Victorian Christmas room off a treat. Suddenly Edith Vogel's piano music drifted up from the basement flat. We lifted our Whisky glasses and Jock said, "Not a bad way to go eh? Mr Basson."

The tenants became as important to me as any of the buildings. A building surveyor is not worth his salt unless he knows how the structure of the building and the components within it work together to satisfy the occupants. My job provided me with a fast track awareness of this joint importance leading to satisfactory accommodation.

After six years the Association decided to split its housing stock into regions so I went to lead a larger regional technical office. Our housing stock increased enormously over the years. I believe today it amounts to many thousands of properties. I ran the regional repairs section for another seven years. Within this time one of my technical officers had bought himself a home computer. He had difficulty detaching himself from it. Fascination would not fully describe his interest; even after the office closed he sat, sometimes until midnight, trying to understand how the software worked it. He was a very capable, intelligent person who, eventually, built my office a computer programme that contained our wish list. What I mean by that is, my staff would make lists of what they would like an office computer to do for them. Within less than a year he had built us the first fully operational office system.

Romance without kisses

It controlled all the daily work going out to various builders.

It printed weekly sheets showing outstanding repair work as yet incomplete.

It controlled our budgets and expenditure and much more.

This came like a miracle to my office, which now we all take for granted. This genius of a man went on to become nationally known as a software consultant; his name was Patrick. I call Patrick a genius because he told me other stories like how, when he was a sous chef working on board a ship in the merchant navy (Yes Patrick had been around), he had decided to learn French, as the head chef was from France. So he obtained a book to assist him with this and he quietly studied the book alone on his bunk for six weeks. He had never used his tongue to try out his French with anyone. One day the head chef accused Patrick of stealing his watch. A violent row went on for half an hour, until thankfully the watch was found by others in the kitchen, during this loud exchange. Patrick still annoyed, went back to his bunk when it suddenly hit him that he could now speak French! His lengthy argument with the chef had all been in the chef's own language.

Patrick's father was a professor whom I had the privilege to meet one day. He wanted a lift so I offered to take him. During this journey his father told me about his other two children. One was a doctor and the other a teacher but, he went on to say, Patrick had never achieved anything with his life. This remark came at a time when his son was an Association star and famous for what he had done for us.

He continued with a smile on his face, "You see, I think my late wife must have dropped him on his head when he was a baby and so damaged his brain."

I looked at him at him in amazement and said, "Don't you know how clever your son really is with computers; he is an expert!"

Patrick's father had no idea how brilliant his son was and I was so pleased to dispel his father's fears about Patrick's brain being damaged.

I had one more advancement in the Association to come. I was sent to the short leasing section of the Association, which leased vacant properties from private owners and leased them back to the Borough of Brent, taking families out of expensive hotels. This received cross-political party agreement. This part of the Association's undertaking ballooned overnight, reaching far above expectations, until at one point it had as many staff as the parent organisation itself. Clearly this quick growth had given rise to many difficult situations. I was chosen to go over and lead this large technical staff of surveyors; many had come from outside employment agencies and some were not at all capable.

I undertook this responsibility with great trepidation. I could not refuse the Chief Executive's desperate requests, as he wanted me to take control of a very dysfunctional Technical department. It took me many months to sort this one out, disposing of staff as I found them unfit for the positions they held. I worked a twelve-hour day, but eventually pulled the department back from the brink of embarrassment.

By this time I had been working for the Association for almost twenty years and my private life had become a mess. So, to save my second marriage I decided to retire early. Later I returned as a consultant but this was not received very well at home. So at the age of 63 I left this work in London; I made the adjustment by buying a set of tools and a Vauxhall van and I became a property developer all over again, but this time with many managerial skills that I had developed.

In my retirement I became an unpaid member of the 'Shaftsbury Housing Trust'. I was appointed as a board member because I knew a lot about looking after their assets, which were their housing stock and their sheltered tenants.

Having had such an unplanned career, something or someone must have been guiding me through to succeed in the end. It could all be put down to coincidences, but there have been too many in my lifetime for this to stack up.

"Gold-dust sprinkled over a good healthy body seems more like it, but whose hand did the sprinkling?"

Chapter 13

Terry at Leisure

As a young lad in London I was a street boy playing outside our home, but when I moved to the country I became a different lad, when the love of nature became one of my delights. We kept chickens and now it is great to help my Grandsons look after their flock of three. I have enjoyed birdwatching and to this day love sitting in my garden room, watching the birds feed and hoping that they will use the nest boxes I have made and placed around the garden.

As youngsters we fished in the river Deben and now I love to take my son, David and the twins for a time fishing on the local canal or the river Avon here in Bath. In 2007 I took a set of lessons learning how to fly fish. The venue for this venture was Chew Valley Lake, a very large reservoir supplying Bristol with its water. It was a great new skill to learn and I put it into practice when we had a holiday in a fishing lodge in the Peak District. What a pleasure it was to catch, cook and eat my trout, all in the space of an afternoon. The same was repeated on a holiday in the Charente area of France when I fished the lake next to the old mill where we stayed. We also fished the lake in Rotorua in New Zealand, but this time the trout was so huge that it fed two of us with plenty to spare. Di and I were leading a group of Brits on a month's holiday and the trip on the lake, a crater of a former volcano, with a local fisherman as our guide, was our choice one afternoon. All of our group had chosen other activities, so we had an afternoon off looking after them and brought home dinner too! It was interesting to see how carefully the Kiwi fisherman gutted the catch, but instead of throwing bits to the birds, placed them into a plastic bag and took them home to incinerate. He gave us one fish, that we had caught, to take to the hotel to be cooked for our supper. The rest were carefully returned to the lake alive. However, before we were able to eat our fish we had to show our day fishing licence to the chef to show we were above the law. Without this it would have been illegal for him to take the fish into his kitchen.

It is also illegal to take fruit into New Zealand; it was interesting to watch how the customs sniffer dogs went all over our luggage before we picked it up from the baggage section. At first I thought the dogs were checking for drugs and when the dog would not move from one of the suitcases it was clear he had found the smell of fruit. This suitcase belonged to one of our party and he was a retired vicar. It turned out that the vicar's wife did have an empty Morrisons' plastic bag in her case; the fruit had all been eaten on the aircraft. What a clever dog it was to have such a fine nose and to have detected this lingering scent.

When Jean died I was lost and didn't know what to do with myself. I had always admired my brother Arthur and his ability to draw so I decided to 'have a go' myself. One thing led to another and I found myself on a painting holiday, booked by my secretary, for two weeks in Cornwall. I trembled at the thought of being on my own on holiday, but the experience turned out to be such a tonic for me. Soon after I tried to have more lessons with a group but found that there was never enough individual time, so I found myself a personal tutor whose name was Ken Back. It was a long drive to and from his studio, but at the end of his course I felt confident to paint alone. I have painted and given away so many pictures, never wanting payment but having the pleasure of seeing them being enjoyed by others. My sons always laughed when they saw my self-portraits as I always painted myself much younger than I was. I do think that as you age, the reflection looking back at you in the mirror is not allowed to tell the true picture. So it was when I used my mirror to help me paint my self-portrait. I have tried to be an honest painter, but the art always turns out my face to be young and handsome!

My tutor not only taught me to paint, but also to appreciate many of the masters of art. It was then that I became familiar with, and loved the work of 'The Bloomsbury Group'. Vanessa Bell and Duncan Grant, in particular, have influenced the work I do today. Like them I have painted pictures on walls, floors, furniture and anywhere that I feel needs a lift of colour. Sadly I did not have these skills during the wartime kitchen days. Was it not for those picture tins from the Canning Factory, the drabness of the war years would have been a little harder to bear.

I have visited Charleston Farmhouse many times to see where the group spent their days in pursuit of their art. When I visit I see their traditional paintings, walls and furniture decorated with their designs and I am transformed into the wonder of what it must have been like, to spend your days in such idyllic surroundings.

The 'Bloomsbury Group' is very much more than just

art. Charleston Farmhouse is where many of the group spent time. Very talented people, in some case geniuses were all part of this group. John Maynard Keynes wrote his book, 'The Consequences of Peace' there and among many famous others, like Clive Bell, Roger Fry, Litton Strachey and Virginia Woolf, they all left DNA within the fabric of this wonderful little farmhouse. The house is now open to the public and I recommend that if you study the story of 'The Bloomsbury Group' before you visit, it will add so much more pleasure to a better understanding of them all.

A few miles up the road is the small village of Berwick where the village Church is a must to visit. Here you can also see the work of these artists. Every inch of the Church is beautifully decorated, from the wooden pulpit to the rood screen, to the white walls where the Nativity scene includes their faces on some of the familiar characters of the stable from more than 2000 years ago. I have included some of my paintings, which were inspired by Charleston Farmhouse and Berwick Church in this book.

Back home, our guest room has a dual role of being our studio and a place where we can entertain visitors. My old tutor used to say that when you are painting, and you don't seem to have any inspiration, your maker will plug himself into you and you will be transformed. Although the work I produce may not always turn out as I wanted it to, I find that when painting I am indeed, 'taken over' and I am lost in this world of creation.

As my friend Di and I both paint, our walls in Bath show something of our efforts. We each secretly jockey for the best walls to display our work; this is all done when the other one is out of the room, followed by waiting for the other's return to see if it will be all changed back again.

Very little dust is ever allowed to settle for long.

I also like to play golf and as I write this at the age of 77, I still enjoy a competitive round of golf at our local golf club. It combines my love of nature, with a bout of exercise and a good pint of Bath Ales at the end! This beautiful course is more like a nature reserve, where we see many birds using the nesting boxes, geese on the lake and in the mornings often a deer or a hare will chase by us.

So I keep myself busy combining all that with the daily chores of living, visiting the wonderful theatre here in Bath, watching my grandsons play football, emailing and attending a local Church too. My life is full and I thank God for giving me such a long one.

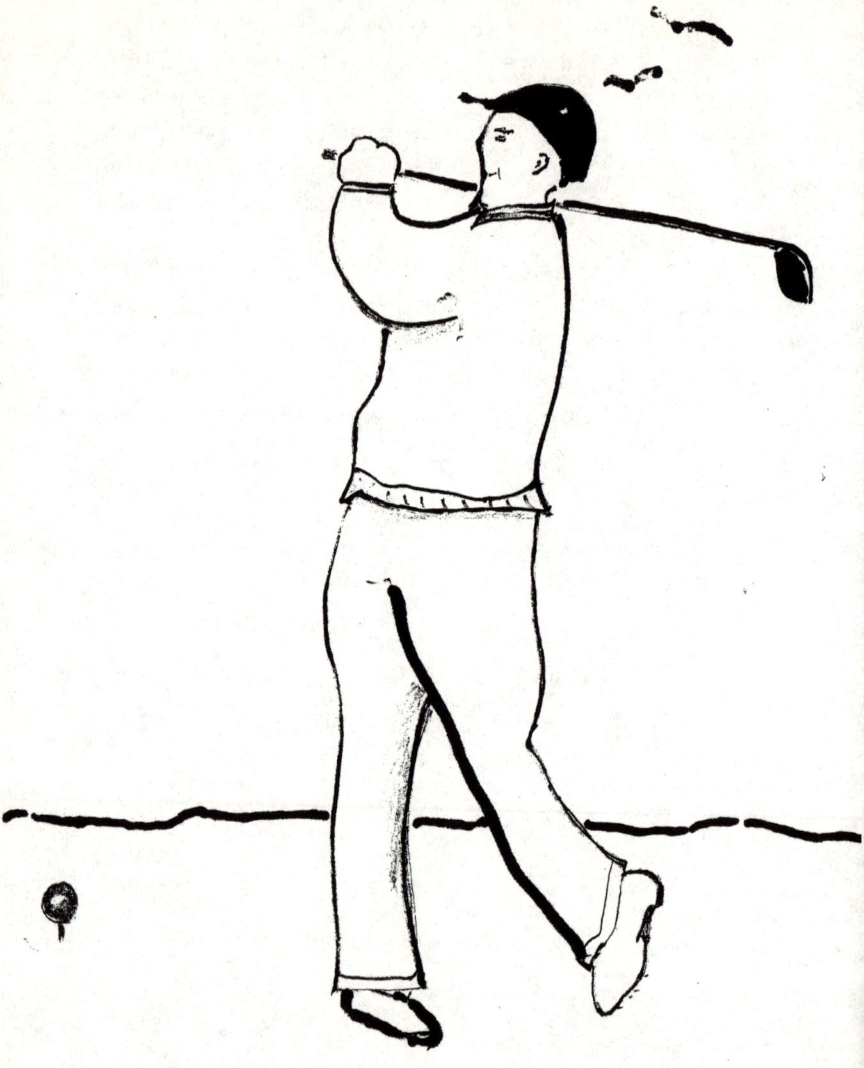

Chapter 14

And Finally!

I now live in Bath, Somerset, a Roman City with a great history. I am still thinking about past times, sharing my home life with my friend Di and enjoying a healthy future, that has been my luck to be experiencing still. My son David, and his family live not a stone's throw away. I have four grandchildren. Twin boys, Saxon and Archie are from David, with two girls, Isobel and Gaby, from my late son Peter.

The War forced the Bassons out of London. My family were Londoners through and through, but the move to the country was to give me the chance to experience ways unknown to me. I treasure this period of my life, which served up all of the things I now hold most dear. My life in Woodbridge showered me with interests. Among many are, wildlife, birdwatching, walks in open green fields, boating on the river and fishing the River Deban. Woodbridge entered my very psyche and has never left me.

On reflection, my book started with the title of **'Romance, without kisses'**, but now, after having written almost all I have to say, I realise that there is evidence of

Romance without kisses

romance without kisses, such as the time with my 'First Love' Joy, my love of nature, the discovery of art, the time in Woodbridge and so much more, but there have also been many kisses on the way because,"I am who I am because of everyone."

"So thank you everyone!"

You know who you are; so I do not need to name all of you, who have guided and helped me through happy and difficult times.

The words in this book could be considered my best attempt to describe how this all came about. I hope I have succeeded.

WW2 memories still hold my fascination. My childhood romance for this wartime period, has given way to much more serious historical research. I feel at times, that I just have to know far more facts about a war, which had to be won. I modelled many wooden Spitfires when I was in Woodbridge.

This year I received a surprise birthday present from Di's son Richard, to accompany him and his family to 'The Fleet Air Arm Museum' at Yeovilton, Somerset. It was a cold day, so he had asked his mum to encourage me to wrap up warm and for her to carry my RAF hat, but to keep it hidden from me. How pleased I was to be wearing my 'Irvin' so I asked him to take a picture of me wearing my flying jacket as a tribute to the few. Out of Di's carrier bag popped my hat so that could be in the picture too! We finally landed up in the museum shop, where I felt a hand behind me stroking my jacket. I turned in the direction of the hand when a man's voice said, "I used to wear one like that."

I asked him if he was a World War Two Spitfire pilot, to which he replied, "I flew Hurricanes."

I showed him my RAF stiff hat, which I had in the carrier bag and which I was now carrying.

"You should walk about the museum wearing it," he said.

For a brief moment I tried it on again, then replied, "I could not walk about the museum in the full kit because I am a fraud standing beside a real hero."

He then introduced me to his wife, whom he had met whilst she was in the WRAF (Women's Royal Air Force).

"I bet she looked great in her uniform?" I said.

With a twinkle in his eye he replied, "She also looked great out of it!"

I wear this same Irvin flying jacket today with pride and respect for all those young men, who flew and died for us in the Battle of Britain.

> "Never in the field of human conflict was so much owed by so many to so few." *Sir Winston Churchill*

On the night of April 14th 2011
in my 77th year,
Joy Marsh came back again
in a Crystal dream.
She came like a Spider riding
her lifeline across a great divide,
Just letting the wind drift her
into my mind.
 Thank you Joy for coming
back to celebrate our
 'Romance Without Kisses'

 Perry Basson.